WADSWORTH PHILOSOPHERS SERIES

ON

DEWEY

The Reconstruction of Philosophy

Robert B. Talisse
Hunter College, The City University of New York

Wadsworth
Thomson Learning™

Australia • Canada • Denmark • Japan • Mexico • New Zealand • Philippines
Puerto Rico • Singapore • Spain • United Kingdom • United States

For Joanne
A pool of clear waters thy mind

Printed in the United States of America
1 2 3 4 5 6 7 03 02 01 00 99

For permission to use material from this text, contact us:
Web: www.thomsonrights.com
Fax: 1-800-730-2215
Phone: 1-800-730-2214

For more information, contact:
Wadsworth/Thomson Learning
10 Davis Drive
Belmont, CA 94002-3098
USA
www.wadsworth.com

ISBN: 0-534-57617-6

Table of Contents

Acknowledgments

The work of a philosopher is no individual affair; it requires the participation of an entire community of inquirers. It would be unfitting for the author of a book about John Dewey to pretend otherwise.

My teachers, now dear friends, Angelo Juffras, Ann Cacoullos, and John Peterman introduced me to American philosophy during my undergraduate years at William Paterson University. I owe much of my philosophical temperament to their influence. I am certain that none will agree with everything I say in the following pages. I nevertheless hope that after reading the book they will be proud to count me as a student.

Similar words of appreciation are due to Bob Gurland of New York University. Portions of the current manuscript draw heavily from seminar papers and a Master's thesis written on Dewey under his direction when I was a graduate student at NYU back in 1994. Bob's talents are legendary among the students at NYU; he is at once a scholar, a philosopher, and a pedagogical phenomenon. As such, he is a living testimony to the power of Dewey's vision. The style and tone of this study owe much to his inspiring example.

The number of debts owed to D. Micah Hester increases steadily. Micah reviewed multiple drafts of every chapter with his characteristic eagerness. This book is without a doubt more graceful in its presentation and much improved in many other respects for his careful attention. Micah also employed his computer skills in formatting the entire text according to Wadsworth's specifications, a task which I am embarrassed to admit is presently beyond my technical abilities. As if these favors were not enough, Micah enlisted the effort of his wife,

Kelly Sherman-Hester, who also read the manuscript and offered a number of suggestions; in particular, Kelly encouraged me to add the summary sections at the end of each substantive chapter. They both get my deepest gratitude.

My colleagues and friends who are philosophers reviewed various parts of the text. Robert Buckley, Keith Burkum, Gregg Caruso, Chalmers Clark, Dwight Goodyear, and Robert Tempio each reviewed parts of the manuscript and offered many helpful comments. Thanks are also due to Steve Cahn, with whom I worked through Dewey's political philosophy at the Graduate School of the City University of New York in the Spring of 1997. Peter Simpson was, as always, very supportive of my efforts.

Non-philosophers of course reviewed the manuscript. My friends, Joanne Billett, Michael Calamari, Matt Cotter, and David McCullough graciously agreed to read the text. They proposed some of the most helpful suggestions regarding the overall presentation of the philosophical issues, and David was especially helpful in the final stages of preparing the text. I have not managed to convince them to take up philosophy professionally, but I hope that they are now better able to appreciate my fascination with the ideas of John Dewey.

Daniel Kolak also deserves acknowledgment. I took an epistemology course with Dan at William Paterson in 1990, and I remember fondly several occasions on which he and I argued over the pragmatic theory of truth. Despite our differences on technical matters (which I suspect are as many as ever), Dan has over the years helped me to understand the value of earnest philosophical engagement. As the general editor of the Wadsworth Philosophy Series, Dan offered several valuable editorial suggestions.

Lastly, I acknowledge those without whose encouragement and support I could hardly have been able to complete this book: Pat Talisse, and Bob Talisse.

Abbreviations

The following abbreviations will be used to indicate the titles of Dewey's major works within the parenthetical citations used throughout this text. Consult the Preface of this volume for a description of the method of citation. Full bibliographical information is provided in the list of suggested reading at the end of the text.

HT	*How We Think* (1910)	(MW6)
	(Revised edition, 1933)	(LW8)
DE	*Democracy and Education* (1916)	(MW9)
RP	*Reconstruction in Philosophy* (1920)	(MW12)
HN	*Human Nature and Conduct* (1922)	(MW14)
EN	*Experience and Nature* (1925)	(LW1)
PP	*The Public and its Problems* (1927)	(LW2)
QC	*The Quest for Certainty* (1929)	(LW4)
IO	*Individualism: Old and New* (1930)	(LW5)
CF	*A Common Faith* (1934)	(LW9)
AE	*Art as Experience* (1934)	(LW10)
LI	*Logic: The Theory of Inquiry* (1938)	(LW12)
EE	*Experience and Education* (1939)	(LW13)
FC	*Freedom and Culture* (1939)	(LW13)

Preface

This little book introduces some major themes in the philosophy of John Dewey. It is intended for students beginning in philosophy and general readers interested in Dewey's thought. Prior training in philosophy has not been assumed of the reader and none is required. I have tried to keep the technical jargon of academic philosophy to a minimum and to always provide sufficient indication of the meanings of technical terms when their use could not be avoided.

In the course of his celebrated career, Dewey offered philosophical treatments of all aspects of human experience: art, knowledge, education, morals, politics, science, and religion. This makes the task of producing a concise yet thorough introductory text particularly challenging. What are the most essential aspects of Dewey's philosophy? As scholarly opinion is divided with regard to this question, each Dewey specialist is likely to find something in the following pages about which to complain. Certainly, there are many ways in which this book could have been written. As one's aspirations must be modest in a text of this length, I have waived the critical appraisals that might otherwise be appropriate for general explications of those traits that are most fundamental to Dewey's philosophical project. I aim to provide an accurate sketch of Dewey's thought which can ground and, more importantly, inspire a more detailed examination of his work. Should I succeed, I have included at the end of the book and in several endnotes suggestions for further study.

A word must be said about Dewey's writings. Dewey's first philosophical essay was published in 1882; the barrage of articles, reviews, and books continued steadily until his death in 1952. The complete writings of John Dewey are published by Southern Illinois University Press in 37 substantial volumes. The volumes are divided into three chronological periods: *The Early Works; The Middle Works;* and *The Later Works*. As they are critical editions, citations to Dewey's works will be keyed to these volumes.

I have slightly revised the convention among Dewey scholars for citing Dewey's works. Quotations are typically cited by parenthetical reference to the period and volume number of the cited *Works* text followed by a colon and the page number. Hence a citation such as (LW1:107) denotes page 107 of the first volume of *The Later Works*. Although standard, this method presents a difficulty. The scholarly convention does not specify by *title* the source of a given quotation. While not a problem for professional scholars with access to the *Works*, this does pose an obstacle to non-specialists who may be using other editions of Dewey's writings. I think it is important for my reader to be able to identify the source of textual quotations by *title*, and not simply by volume number in the *Works*. When quoting from a major work, then, I have included an abbreviated form of the title within the parenthetical citation; hence a citation such as (*EN*, LW1:107) indicates that the quotation occurs on page 107 of the first volume of *The Later Works*, which is Dewey's book, *Experience and Nature*. When citing from essays or from minor works, I have tried to indicate within the text the titles from which the quotations come. Please consult the list of abbreviations on page iii of this volume.

In his masterpiece on education, *Democracy and Education*, Dewey claims that a student's first encounter with a new subject should be "as unscholastic as possible" (*DE*, MW9:161). I hope my presentation amounts to something more than merely a textbook report of the central points in Dewey's philosophy. Noting also Dewey's insistence that "thinking occurs when things are uncertain or doubtful or problematic" (*DE*, MW9:155), I have tried throughout to engage the reader philosophically; that is, I have endeavored to place Dewey's ideas within the context of the philosophical problems to which they were developed to respond. Setting the philosophical stage takes time and care, and I hope the reader's patience is not too often put to the test. I'd like to think that upon completion of this text, the reader would not only have gained an understanding of John Dewey's philosophy, but an appreciation for philosophy itself.

1
Introduction

Who is John Dewey?

John Dewey is arguably the greatest American philosopher. To say that Dewey is an American philosopher is not to simply state a geographical fact; there is something distinctively *American* in Dewey's philosophy. In his lifetime, he was hailed as "*the* philosopher of American democracy." Writing just prior to Dewey's death, historian Henry Commager offered the following estimation:

> So faithfully did Dewey live up to his own philosophical creed that he became the guide, the mentor, and the conscience of the American people; it is scarcely an exaggeration to say that for a generation no issue was clarified until Dewey had spoken.[1]

On the occasion of Dewey's death, former student and close friend Sidney Hook wrote of Dewey:

> He leaves behind him no monument in stone, no empire, fortune or foundation. Yet his bequest is immense and imponderable. The experience of millions of American children is richer and happier for his having lived. And to every adult mind he has offered a reasoned and reasonable faith by which to live.[2]

These accolades should not suggest that Dewey was not a controversial figure. As one might expect, not everyone shared Hook and Commager's the enthusiasm for Dewey. Critics saw in Dewey's philosophy a dangerous fascination with science and technology and a radical vision of extreme democracy. According to one critic:

> Dewey's philosophy . . . constitutes an attempt to destroy all philosophy. Dewey has made America lose its perspective and has thus greatly weakened the intellectual potential of American leadership at home and abroad.[3]

Despite Dewey's centrality to the American intellectual and political scene during his lifetime, today surprisingly little is known of John Dewey outside academic circles. As Dewey's ideas continue to exert considerable influence upon American life, his current obscurity is lamentable. We shall thus begin with some biographical remarks.[4]

John Dewey was born a grocer's son in Burlington, Vermont on October 20, 1859. A bashful boy, the young Dewey spent his early years in the company of his elder and more gregarious brother, Davis. Although they disliked school, the Dewey boys were bookish and contemplative; they worked delivering newspapers to earn money to purchase books. When not reading, the pair enjoyed the opportunities for adventure offered by Lake Champlain and the Green Mountains, animated with the frontier spirit. Camping and fishing trips were frequent; it is likely that the intense reverence for nature characteristic of Dewey's thought has its source in these early experiences.

Dewey entered the University of Vermont in September of 1875, just prior to his sixteenth birthday. The University curriculum was of the traditional sort; students took courses in Greek and Latin, mathematics, history, and natural science. Although philosophy was reserved for the final year of study, a junior year course in T. H. Huxley's *Elements of Physiology* aroused "a distinctive philosophic interest" in Dewey (LW5:148). In Huxley's text, Dewey encountered a comprehensive vision of nature that emphasized the organic unity of the creature, the symbiotic relation of organism and environment, and the continuum of life. Against the background of Dewey's Congregational upbringing which stressed the separation "of self from the world, of soul from body, of nature from God" (LW5:153), Huxley's view represented the possibility of intellectual liberation. Dewey reports of his engagement with physiology:

> . . . there was derived from that study a sense of interdependence and interrelated unity that gave form to intellectual stirrings that had been previously inchoate, and created a kind of type or model to which material in any field ought to conform. . . . I was led to desire a world and a life that would have the same properties as had the human organism in the picture of it derived from study of Huxley's treatment. (LW5:147-148)

Dewey turned to philosophy in the hopes of finding an image of the world and Man's place in nature that exhibited the virtues he saw in Huxley. As we will soon discover, Dewey's desire was fulfilled by his own philosophy; the vocabulary and categories of biology—environment, organism, interaction, continuity—and a stern resistance to supernaturalism and dualism permeate Dewey's thinking.

At the time of Dewey's first encounter with academic philosophy, the discipline in America was still closely related to theology, and most of the philosophy instructors were clergymen. The reigning philosophy then was intuitionism. According to this school, the fundamental tenets of logic, metaphysics, and ethics can be grasped directly by the human mind's faculty of 'intuition', independently of sensory experience. That this principle inevitably leads to a dualistic view of the world is easy to see. Those principles which can be grasped through intuition are of a kind distinct from those which require confirmation via sensory experience; consequently, the *objects* of the former kind of principle are taken to be distinct from those of the latter. Intuitionism thus retained many of the standard philosophical dualisms from which Dewey was trying to escape; on the view of the intuitionists, mind is separate from body, experience from intuition, fact from value, and reason from science.

It is not surprising that intuitionism should have been amiable to clergymen. Apart from the fact that Western religion thrives upon dualism of various sorts, the intuitionists placed principal theological doctrines concerning God and the soul firmly among the self-verifying truths known by human intuition. They were thus established beyond doubt, safely out of the reach of the scientific skepticism nurtured by *empiricism*, the view that maintains that all knowledge comes through sense experience. Alluding to the profound vision of unity he found in Huxley, Dewey recalls learning "the terminology of an intuitional philosophy," but acknowledges that "it did not go deep, and in no way did it satisfy what I was dimly reaching for" (LW5:149).

After graduation, Dewey took a position teaching high school in South Oil City, Pennsylvania. He stayed there for two years, teaching Latin, algebra, and science for forty dollars a month. Although Dewey had no formal training in teaching, his University courses prepared him well in these subjects. Throughout his time in Oil City, Dewey read voraciously in philosophy. His interest in physiology led him to the intellectual debates surrounding the philosophical implications of the theory of evolution and, ultimately, to metaphysics.[5]

Just prior to the end of the academic year 1881, Dewey wrote a philosophical essay titled "The Metaphysical Assumptions of Materialism" (EW1). He sent the essay to W. T. Harris, editor of the *Journal of Speculative Philosophy*, along with a note asking Harris to honestly assess the philosophical talents of its author.[6] Returning to Burlington in June of 1881, Dewey took a temporary teaching position at the Lake View Seminary Academy and waited to hear from Harris.

Back in Burlington, Dewey reestablished contact with his philosophy teacher from college, H. A. P. Torrey. Under Torrey's private instruction, Dewey studied the classic texts in philosophy and learned to read German. With Torrey's encouragement, and a salutary response from Harris—who accepted Dewey's essay for publication[7]—Dewey resolved to pursue a career in philosophy. Dewey began graduate work in philosophy at the Johns Hopkins University in September of 1882.

At Hopkins, Dewey fell under the influence of Professor George Sylvester Morris, who taught in the Hopkins philosophy department as a visiting professor from the University of Michigan. Morris introduced Dewey to the absolute idealism of German philosopher, G. W. F. Hegel (1770-1831). On Hegel's view, philosophical dualisms are but temporary moments within a larger unity that is coming to be. This comprehensive unity, which Hegel called *Geist* ("Spirit"), is gradually realized through History. Hegel's philosophy was therefore thoroughly anti-dualistic; he understood life, ideas, and nature to exist within the development of *Geist.*

With its emphasis on synthesis and continuity, Hegel's system contrasted sharply with the intuitionism Dewey learned at the University of Vermont. In Hegel's philosophy, Dewey found what he had been "dimly reaching for" since his college days. Hegel healed the "inward laceration" left by Dewey's upbringing; absolute idealism satisfied Dewey's "intense emotional craving" for a philosophical articulation of continuity (LW5:153). Although Dewey eventually abandoned the abstruse jargon and idealistic metaphysics of Hegelianism for a perspective of his own design called "empirical naturalism" (*EN*, LW1:10) or "experimentalism," the encounter with Hegel "left a permanent deposit" in his thinking (LW5:154).

Dewey completed the Ph. D. in 1884 with a dissertation on "The Psychology of Kant."[8] He accepted an offer from Morris to join the philosophy department at the University of Michigan in Ann Arbor as an assistant professor. At Michigan, Dewey taught courses in ethics, history of philosophy, logic, and psychology. His courses lead to the publication of several articles as well as his first book. Dewey's *Psychology* (EW2) appeared in 1887. In the *Psychology*, Dewey tried to demonstrate that the findings of scientific psychology confirmed the idealistic metaphysics of Hegel. Although the book was subjected to harsh criticism, it earned Dewey significant scholarly notice. A second book, a study of the philosophy of Leibniz, appeared the next year.[9]

As a result of his impressive record of publication, Dewey was invited to join the faculty of the University of Minnesota as Professor of Mental and Moral Philosophy in 1888. Dewey moved to Minnesota in the Fall of 1888; however, his stay there was brief. He returned to Ann Arbor in 1889 to fill the position of Chair of the Philosophy Department, which was vacated when Morris died in 1888.[10] Dewey's most pressing task upon his arrival in Michigan was to appoint an assistant philosophy professor. Dewey hired James Hayden Tufts, a man with whom Dewey would write an influential textbook on ethics and who would become an important philosopher in his own right.[11]

During his second period at Michigan Dewey's thinking began to shift decisively away from Hegelianism. Instrumental to this shift was Dewey's study of William James's 1890 classic, *The Principles of Psychology*. Like Dewey, James rejected the dualistic categories of traditional philosophy; however, unlike Dewey, James did not take refuge in the idealistic metaphysics of Hegel. Instead, James sought continuity by way of the functionalism implicit in evolutionary biology. Dewey used James's text in his 1891 seminar; according to Dewey, the *Principles* initiated a "new direction and quality" (LW5:157) in his thought. Dewey's work throughout the early 1890s attests to James's influence.[12]

On the recommendation of Tufts, who had left Michigan for Chicago in 1893, Dewey was offered the head professorship in philosophy at the University of Chicago in 1894. Dewey's decade at Chicago was eventful and hence marks a crucial phase in his intellectual development; during this period Dewey's own philosophy begins to emerge. At Chicago, Dewey's interests broadened; he published several important articles in areas he had previously not fully explored such as logical theory, social philosophy, and epistemology. By his second year at Chicago, Dewey had assembled a stable and impressive philosophy department.[13] In 1903 there appeared a collection of articles written by the Chicago Philosophy Department titled *Studies in Logical Theory*.[14] Although the *Studies* reflects a diversity of philosophical interests among its authors, it represents the cooperative development of a distinctive philosophical perspective. In his 1904 review of the *Studies*, William James wrote:

> Professor John Dewey, and at least ten of his disciples, have collectively put into the world a statement . . . of a view of the world. . . which is so simple, massive, and positive that . . . it deserves the title of a new system of philosophy.[15]

Collectively, the authors of *Studies in Logical Theory* came to be known as the "Chicago School" or the "Chicago Pragmatists"[16] and John Dewey was undisputedly their leader.

It is also during his tenure at Chicago that Dewey became interested in educational theory. The Chicago philosophy department was responsible for the University's offerings in pedagogy. Dewey seized this opportunity to bring his psychological and philosophical views to the test. In 1895, Dewey had secured the requisite funding and permissions to open an elementary school to be run under the auspices of the Chicago philosophy department. The "University Elementary School," later called the "Laboratory School," and popularly known as the "Dewey School" flourished for nearly eight years.[17] Dewey's experiences with the Laboratory School helped him to develop the comprehensive philosophy of education for which he is well known. His early foray into the philosophy of education led to the publication of several seminal articles on education and two short books which are still regarded as classics: *The School and Society* (MW1) and *The Child and the Curriculum* (MW2).

Dewey's efforts turned to social activism during his Chicago years. Shortly after arriving in Chicago, Dewey established relations with Jane Addams and her social settlement, Hull House. Dewey served on the first board of trustees of Hull House and he offered lectures and lead group discussions on pressing social issues. His experience at Hull House would have a lasting impact upon his thinking; Dewey would come to adopt the position that the philosopher must be constantly engaged with the issues facing society at large and that philosophy is essentially social criticism.

Differences with the University surrounding the Laboratory School drove Dewey to leave Chicago in 1904. He joined the Department of Philosophy and Psychology at Columbia University in New York City in February of 1905. While at Columbia, Dewey continued the comprehensive philosophical project begun at Chicago, publishing a series of books and articles that are today placed among the most important works of twentieth-century philosophy. Through association with Columbia Teachers College, Dewey continued his work in education theory. This work produced in 1911 the influential *How We Think* (MW6) and in 1916 his masterpiece of educational philosophy, *Democracy and Education* (MW9).[18] Dewey was quickly recognized as the leader of the 'progressive movement' in education, and is still considered an important educational theorist.

By the time of his retirement from teaching in 1930, the catalogue of Dewey's accomplishments was astonishingly extensive. He lectured in Japan in 1919, in China in 1920, and in 1929 he delivered the Gifford Lectures at the University of Edinburgh, which were subsequently published as his major work in epistemology, *The Quest for Certainty* (LW4).[19] His invited lectures in the United States resulted in the publication of several major books including *Human Nature and Conduct* (1922; MW14), *Experience and Nature* (1925; LW1), and *The Public and Its Problems* (1926; LW2).

Dewey's activities were not restricted to the academy, however. By request of the Turkish government, Dewey visited Turkey in 1924 to evaluate the educational system; he produced a comprehensive report and made a number of suggestions that were adopted. He was invited to the Soviet Union for the same purpose in 1928.[20] Additionally, Dewey helped found the American Association of University Professors and the National Association for the Advancement of Colored People; he was instrumental in organizing the American Civil Liberties Union, participated in the struggle for women's suffrage, led a movement to outlaw war, and headed organizations of political activism.[21]

Dewey's retirement from teaching did not mark a retreat from philosophical and political involvement. As Columbia University Professor Emeritus in Residence, Dewey produced some of his most important philosophical work. In 1931 he delivered the first William James Lecture at Harvard University, which would become his seminal work in aesthetics, *Art As Experience* (1934; LW10). In his Terry Foundation Lectures at Yale in 1934, Dewey developed the controversial philosophy of religion which would be published as *A Common Faith* (LW9). Two significant books on political philosophy appeared in the 1930s: *Liberalism and Social Action* (1935; LW11) and *Freedom and Culture* (1938; LW13). And 1938 brought the publication of Dewey's *magnum opus* synthesizing logical theory and scientific methodology, *Logic: The Theory of Inquiry* (LW12).

On the political front, Dewey tirelessly worked to promote democracy. He called for the organization of a third political party that would address the concerns of Americans in the grip of the depression.[22] He wrote hundreds of articles, delivered radio addresses, and spoke before political organizations throughout the country.

In what was perhaps his greatest show of political courage, Dewey in 1937, at the age of seventy-eight, traveled to Mexico City to chair the hearings of the Commission of Inquiry into the Charges Made against Leon Trotsky in the Moscow Trials. Although Dewey harbored no sympathies with Trotsky's ideology, he believed the Soviet exile was entitled to a fair trial. Dewey's decision to participate in the Inquiry was met with harsh and sometimes cruel criticism from the American Communist press, whose support for Stalin's regime was boundless. Whereas Stalin had tried and convicted Trotsky and his son *in absentia* during a series of political trials in 1936 and 1937, the "Dewey Commission," as it came to be known, found Leon Trotsky and his son not guilty of treason and murder, as Stalin had alleged.[23] History has vindicated the findings of the Dewey Commission; it is now universally acknowledged that Stalin's trials were nothing short of an official purge of all political opposition to Stalin's rule.

In 1940, Dewey would again enter the fray of political controversy in defense of the principles of a free society. In February of 1940, the City College of New York announced the appointment of the renowned and controversial British philosopher, Bertrand Russell to a distinguished chair in the Philosophy Department. Russell was notorious for his atheism and his non-traditional views regarding sex and marriage. Notice of Russell's appointment sparked outcries from various quarters of the religious community, culminating in an especially incendiary letter to the *New York Times* by Episcopalian Bishop William Manning. As opposition grew, pressure was placed on the College to withdraw Russell's appointment. Although Dewey and Russell could hardly be called philosophical allies, Dewey, along with the Committee for Cultural Freedom (a civil liberties group he helped found in 1939), rose to Russell's defense. Arguing that Russell's opponents had no right to silence him, Dewey urged critics to instead attempt to address Russell's views in the forum of open debate.[24]

Sadly, a lawsuit brought before the New York Supreme Court in March of 1940 resulted in the official rescinding of Russell's appointment at the City College. Of this, Dewey wrote in a personal letter: "If groups of the Ancient Order of Hiberians plus Bishop Manning are going to dictate who shall and shan't teach philosophy in American colleges, I'm glad I haven't much time left."[25] As it turned out, Dewey had more time than he might have expected. In 1949, his ninetieth year, Dewey co-authored (with Arthur Bentley) his last full-length philosophical work, *Knowing and the Known* (LW16).

John Dewey died of pneumonia in New York City on June 1st, 1952. At the time of his death, Dewey was still regularly publishing articles, contributing essays and reviews, and undertaking political action. Although today we are accustomed to thinking of academics—especially philosophers—as aloof spectators upon the real world, these remarks show that there is at least one compelling counter-example to this common, and often justified, perception. Dewey's was not a life of detached contemplation, but of constant and directed action.

A Sketch of Pragmatism

John Dewey's thought is most commonly associated with the philosophical movement known as pragmatism.[26] The only philosophical movement indigenous to America, pragmatism remains one of the most controversial products of twentieth century philosophy. Although a detailed examination of pragmatism lies beyond the scope of our current study, a few remarks are in order about the origins of pragmatism and some of its principal characteristics.[27]

According to Charles Sanders Peirce (1839-1914), the man who founded the pragmatism movement, the philosophical idea he would call "pragmatism" was proposed by him at the meetings of an informal philosophy group that met in Cambridge, Massachusetts in the early 1870s which called itself the Metaphysical Club.[28] Drawing upon the discussions of the Metaphysical Club, Peirce composed two articles, "The Fixation of Belief" and "How To Make Our Ideas Clear," which are today thought to mark the birth of the pragmatism. These essays were published in the *Popular Science Monthly* in the years 1877 and 1878, respectively.

Peirce's "Fixation" and "Ideas" articles are today considered among the most important in philosophy; however, they received little attention at the time of their publication. Pragmatism lay dormant until William James (1842-1910) made use of Peirce's ideas in a 1898 address titled "Philosophical Conceptions and Practical Results." In this essay, James credits Peirce with first proposing the principle of pragmatism, while insisting that Peirce's formulation is too narrow. James's broadened variety of pragmatism was given full expression in a series of 1906 lectures, published in 1907 with the title *Pragmatism: A New Name for Some Old Ways of Thinking*. By this time, the pragmatic movement was growing steadily, winning adherents in England, France, and Italy.[29]

Whereas Peirce's writings went largely unnoticed by the philosophical community, James's pragmatism sparked remarkable controversy. *Pragmatism* precipitated a flurry of critiques, objections, and supposed refutations from various thinkers, including two eminent British philosophers, G. E. Moore and Bertrand Russell. According to many critics, James's philosophy was an unabashed assertion of the vulgarities of American commercialism.[30]

Although the controversy surrounding James's expression of pragmatism led both Peirce and Dewey to abandon the term,[31] today the three thinkers are often discussed collectively, and James's *Pragmatism* is still considered the principal expression of pragmatist philosophy. Pragmatism, in its various forms, remained an influential philosophical perspective throughout Dewey's life; however, interest in pragmatist philosophy dropped dramatically in the 1950s as a new style of philosophizing, "philosophical analysis," came into prominence. Since the 1980s, however, there has been growing steadily a "neo-pragmatist" movement among philosophers in America. Contemporary figures such as Hilary Putnam, Richard Rorty, and Cornel West have put the insights of the original pragmatists to work with in the contexts of current philosophical debate.[32] Not unlike that of their philosophical forefathers, the work of the neo-pragmatists has met with thorough criticism.[33] Nonetheless, the ideas of Charles Sanders Peirce, William James, and John Dewey are once again at the center of philosophical discussion and debate.

As is often the case with intellectual movements involving figures of great originality, it is difficult to identify philosophical theses that pragmatists share. We may, however, catalogue a few tendencies and motifs that are characteristically pragmatist. These tendencies will be evident in the discussion of Dewey to come.

1. *Dissatisfaction with traditional philosophy.* Pragmatism represents an *alternative* to traditional ways of philosophizing. The pragmatists argue that the traditional vocabularies and problems of philosophy are obsolete or otherwise disposable. As Peirce wrote to James in a 1904 letter, "Pragmatism solves no real problems. It only shows that the supposed problems are not real problems." Pragmatism thus offers a new conception of philosophy, a new philosophical vocabulary, and a new series of philosophical problems.

2. *Emphasis upon Action.* Pragmatist efforts to develop a new *kind* of philosophy share a concern for action. Whereas traditional philosophies had prized the image of the detached contemplator, pragmatism urges the importance of human *behavior.*

3. *Anti-intellectualism.* Pragmatist emphases upon action are, most generally, manifestations of an attitude we may call 'anti-intellectualism'. That is, pragmatists are suspicious of any philosophical theory or idea that is supposed to be of exclusively "intellectual" concern. According to pragmatists, the significance of an idea or theory lies in its implications for the behavior of human beings in the world of everyday affairs. Accordingly, the pragmatists insist that philosophy must *accomplish* something, it must speak to the concerns of the world at large.

4. *Desire to make philosophy more scientific.* Traditional philosophers have thought that part of their job was to provide the theoretical foundations of natural science; in this sense, science was to *conform* to the requirements set by the philosophers. Pragmatists, by contrast, reject this project. Instead, pragmatists attempt to bring philosophy more in line with the practices of the sciences by insisting that philosophical ideas be evaluated according to methods of the sort employed in scientific inquiry.

5. *Reconciliation of science and value.* Pragmatists understand that the accomplishments of science pose a problem for values. Could human values find a place in the cold, purposeless universe of modern science? Pragmatists thus attempt to recast traditional accounts of value and traditional accounts of science into terms that allow reconciliation of the two.

The Plan of this Study

Although each chapter in this book is focused upon a different aspect of Dewey's philosophy, no chapter can be profitably read independently of its predecessors. Like Dewey's philosophy, this study exhibits a certain systematic quality, and the general theme of Dewey's attempt to *reconstruct* philosophy is developed throughout. Earlier chapters thus provide the groundwork for later discussions, and later discussions tend to shed light upon earlier points; I have tried to make such connections explicit within the body of the text. As I shall cover a lot of philosophical ground in only a little space, it may be best to lay out a general outline of what is to come.

I begin with an examination of Dewey's radical conception of philosophy. Dewey is one of the handful of major thinkers who has taken *metaphilosophy* (viz., philosophical questions concerning the very nature of philosophy itself) seriously. Dewey's metaphilosophical investigations have produced a series of powerful criticisms of traditional philosophy as well as a plan to correct, revise, and reconstruct that tradition. As Dewey's philosophy is an attempt to recover the true philosophical enterprise, the metaphilosophical context is essential.

The elementary category for all of Dewey's thought is experience. Dewey's theory of experience is the subject of Chapter Three. A proper examination of Dewey's concept of experience will require a bit of stage setting, and I trust the reader will not object to a brief lesson in the history of philosophy. Although Dewey is an empiricist, he rejects the conception of experience associated with the British empiricist school of the 17th and 18th centuries. This theory of experience, perhaps best expressed in the work of John Locke (1632 - 1704), led to a series of epistemological puzzles and, ultimately, to the skepticism of David Hume (1711 - 1776). Dewey's Darwinian view of experience follows from his metaphilosophical principle that philosophy must align itself with the natural sciences.

The radically empirical theory of experience that Dewey formulates underlies his rejection of traditional epistemology and informs his positive account of knowledge. In Chapter Four, I examine Dewey's rejection of what he called the "spectator theory of knowledge." A reconstructed epistemology substitutes the spectator view with an experimental theory of knowing according to which knowing is 'inquiry', a certain pattern of behavior.

In Chapter Five, I show how Dewey's reconstructed conceptions of experience and knowing inform his social vision. The study closes with some brief remarks about the significance of Dewey's philosophy for how we live our lives.

Endnotes

[1] Commager, *The American Mind* (New Haven: Yale University Press, 1950), 100.

[2] Hook, "Some Memories of John Dewey," reprinted in his *Pragmatism and the Tragic Sense of Life* (New York: Basic Books, 1974), 101.

[3] Crosser, Paul K. *The Nihilism of John Dewey* (New York: Philosophical Books, 1955), ix.

[4] The account which follows is drawn mainly from Dewey's brief autobiographical essay, "From Absolutism to Experimentalism" (LW5: 147-160), Jane Dewey's "Biography of John Dewey" (in Schilpp, ed. *The Philosophy of John Dewey*, Illinois: Open Court,

1989), and Dykhuizen's *The Life and Mind of John Dewey* (Illinois: Southern Illinois University Press, 1973).
[5] *Metaphysics* is the area of philosophy which examines questions concerning the most fundamental aspects of Reality.
[6] Dewey's letter is reproduced in Dykhuizen, *ibid.*, 23.
[7] "The Metaphysical Assumptions of Materialism" appeared in the *Journal of Speculative Philosophy* in June of 1882. A second article by Dewey, "The Pantheism of Spinoza" (EW1), appeared in the July issue of the same year.
[8] The dissertation was never published and has been lost. An 1884 essay, "Kant and Philosophic Method" (EW1), is believed to reflect the main contentions of Dewey's doctoral thesis.
[9] *Leibniz's New Essays on Human Understanding* (EW1).
[10] As indicated in Dewey's memorial, "The Late Professor Morris" (EW3), the passing of Morris affected Dewey rather deeply.
[11] The *Ethics* by Dewey and Tufts was published in 1908 (MW5); a revised version was published in 1932 (LW7).
[12] See Dewey's 1894 article "The Theory of Emotion" (EW4).
[13] In addition to Tufts, the department included George Herbert Mead, whose work in social psychology is still well regarded.
[14] Dewey's contributions to this volume may be found in MW2.
[15] William James, "The Chicago School," reprinted in his *Essays in Philosophy* (Cambridge: Harvard University Press, 1978), 102.
[16] Pragmatism will be discussed in the next section of this chapter.
[17] See Mayhew and Edwards, *The Dewey School* (New York: D. Appleton-Century, 1936) for the history of the Dewey school.
[18] A revised edition of *How We Think* appeared in 1933 (LW8).
[19] His lectures in Japan were published in 1920 as *Reconstruction In Philosophy* (MW12). He wrote several essays about China, all of which are collected in MW 11.
[20] Dewey's report on the Turkish educational system is included in MW 15. His report on Russian education is compiled in LW3.
[21] Robert Westbrook's *John Dewey and American Democracy* (Ithaca: Cornell University Press, 1991) and Alan Ryan's *John Dewey and the High Tide of American Liberalism* (New York: W. W. Norton, 1995) nicely canvass Dewey's political involvement.

[22] Several articles, essays, and addresses concerning these matters are compiled in LW6.
[23] A complete report of the findings of the Commission was published as *Not Guilty!* (New York: Monad Press, 1938).
[24] Dewey's "The Case for Bertrand Russell" is in LW14. See also Dewey and Kallen, eds., *The Bertrand Russell Case* (New York: Viking Press, 1941).
[25] Reproduced in Dykhuizen, *ibid.*, 306.
[26] According to William James, the term 'pragmatism' derives from the Greek *pragma,* which means "action." James, *Pragmatism* (Massachusetts: Harvard University Press, 1975), 28.
[27] H. S. Thayer's *Meaning and Action* (Indianapolis: Hackett, 1981) is the best critical study of classical pragmatism available. See also John P. Murphy's *Pragmatism: From Peirce to Davidson* (Colorado: Westview Press, 1990) and H. O. Mounce's *The Two Pragmatisms: From Peirce to Rorty* (New York: Routledge, 1997).
[28] For Peirce's account of the origin of pragmatism, see paragraphs 11–13 in volume five of *The Collected Papers of Charles Sanders Peirce* (Cambridge: Harvard University Press, 8 vols. 1931-1958).
[29] See Thayer, *ibid.,* Part Four.
[30] On this criticism, see Dewey's "Pragmatic America" (MW13).
[31] In 1905, Peirce rebaptized his philosophy "pragmaticism," a name he hoped would be "ugly enough to be safe from kidnappers" (*ibid.,* paragraph 414). Dewey's critical review James's *Pragmatism* is titled "What Pragmatism Means by Practical." It is included in MW4 and also in Hester and Talisse eds., *Dewey's Essays in Experimental Logic* (Carbondale: Southern Illinois University Press, 1999).
[32] See Putnam's *Pragmatism* (New York: Blackwell, 1995); Rorty's *Philosophy and the Mirror of Nature* (New Jersey: Princeton University Press, 1979); and West's *The American Evasion of Philosophy* (Wisconsin: University of Wisconsin Press, 1989).
[33] The main lines of the current debate are represented in the essays collected in Morris Dickstein, ed. *The Revival of*

Pragmatism (Durham: Duke University Press, 1998). See also Saatkamp, ed. *Rorty and Pragmatism* (Tennessee: Vanderbilt University Press, 1995).

2
Reconstructing Philosophy

With the necessary groundwork in place, we now are ready to delve into the mind of John Dewey. Before we embark, I must comment on the narrative strategy I shall employ. In the following pages, we shall not merely *talk about* philosophy, we shall think philosophically. William James has said that philosophies are "visions," they are "modes of feeling the whole push, and seeing the whole drift of life."[1] A textbook survey of Dewey's ideas is therefore inadequate. If we are truly to capture Dewey's vision—his distinctive way of understanding the "drift of life"—we must attempt to confront the problems that generated his ideas, we must *do* philosophy. It is fitting, then, that we begin with a chapter on philosophy itself.

We discovered at the end of the last chapter that pragmatists typically are critical of traditional ways of philosophizing, and consequently wish to propose a new *kind* of philosophy. Dewey is a typical pragmatist in this regard; he aims to *reconstruct* philosophy. The concept of philosophical reconstruction courses throughout all of Dewey's work, and thus is essential to understanding his philosophy. What does it mean to *reconstruct* philosophy? Dewey argues that philosophy itself needs to be refocused; philosophers need to subject their ideas about *what philosophy is* to philosophical scrutiny, they must *question* the enterprise of philosophy itself! Dewey does not simply dismiss traditional philosophy, rather he deploys a philosophical *critique* of philosophy; he devises an argument to show that traditional philosophical problems ought to be abandoned and that new problems ought to be addressed.

Central to Dewey's critique of the philosophical tradition is his *metaphilosophy*, his theory regarding the nature, origin, and objectives of philosophy.[2] We begin with Dewey's account of how philosophies arise, we turn then to his critique of the tradition and finally to his basic strategy for reconstructing philosophy.

The Sources of Philosophy

The Problem: A Live Creature in an Aleatory World

> Man finds himself living in an aleatory world; his existence involves, to put it baldly, a gamble. The world is a scene of risk; it is uncertain, unstable . . . . (*EN,* LW1:43)

As I sit in my study typing this sentence into my computer, the hum of the cars driving on the street below my window is almost loud enough to drown out the chirping of the birds roosting on the telephone wires and in the branches of the nearby trees. The singing of the birds oddly compliments the music that softly plays from the stereo across the room. It is a warm, clear day, the windows are open, and a cool breeze drifts through the apartment, blowing my notes off the top of my desk. Retrieving the scattered papers, I notice the Sun shining brightly through my window; I shall have to draw the blinds if the glare from the Sun gets too intense. If I draw the blinds, however, I shall have to close the windows, and thereby shut out the cool breeze. Perhaps then I will also have to use the air-conditioning to keep the room at a comfortable temperature, for if the room gets too hot, my computer will malfunction and I will have to stop working.

It occurs to me that my writing is taking place amidst a curious composite of natural and technological factors dynamically combined. The cars, the birds, the telephone lines, the trees, the computer, the music, the Sun, and I are all implicated in a common environment. My activity—the writing—must be coordinated with the other factors, or it will be disturbed. But where is the risk, the uncertainty that Dewey claims is an essential trait of the world?

We do not often interrupt the flow of our daily activity to notice the *environment*, the particular set of conditions under which we act. We do not typically think of our actions as occurring within any particular context at all; we *simply* act, we *do something*. We overlook the essential interrelatedness of the world and ourselves. We tend to imagine that there is an insuperable divide between our "inner" selves and the "external" world, with behavior at best constituting the interface between these separate realms. But, on Dewey's view, we are essentially *creatures* living not merely *in* an environment, but *by means of* an environment (*LI*, LW12:32). Our *living* occurs not simply *under* certain conditions, we live *within* those conditions; we do not merely act *upon* the world, we are agents *of* the world.

The environment is thus a fundamental factor. One might say that we literally could not live without the environment. Although true, this way of speaking can mislead. The term 'the environment' can suggest that there is some external and static *entity* upon which our lives depend. This suggestion may encourage us to overlook two facts: (1) the environment is *not* an entity which exists strictly outside of us, we are *part of* the environment, we live *within* it; and (2) the environment is *not* static, it is *processive*, it is *mutable*, it is *dynamic*. The term 'environment' does not denote some permanent, independent entity; rather, it is shorthand for an array of interrelated and active *forces* or *factors* that collectively constitute the *conditions* within which we, at some particular time and in some particular place, live.

We are not accustomed to thinking of ourselves and the world in this way, so let's press the point a bit further. You are now reading a sentence in this book. The activity of reading can occur only if certain environmental conditions prevail; without sufficient light and quiet, for example, reading is impossible. Stop reading for a moment and survey your surroundings. *Where* are you? What are the forces operative within the environment which affect your reading? Is it possible to draw a hard and fast distinction between *you* and the surrounding conditions?

We often think that we exist somewhere *inside* our skin. Is this plausible? Inside your skin there are organs, bones, muscles, plasma, and cells which cooperate in various ways to promote survival. These seemingly inner operations are actually *interactions* with aspects of an environment. When we breathe, for example, we remove air from the environment. The respiratory system then separates the oxygen from the other constituent gases; the oxygen is retained whereas the others are expelled back into the environment. Similar descriptions could be given for every other vital function. In a very literal sense, you are within the environment and the environment is within you. Your skin is not a barrier separating you from the environment. Rather, your skin, like the rest of your body, is continuous with the environment. You are an *organism*, that is, the locus of certain *processes*, a continuous *exchange*, a *transaction* occurring with other forces within an environment. Far from a detached spectator on the world, you are a live creature within the world.[3]

Your survival depends upon the character of the transaction you conduct with other features of the environment. For example, if the environment contains an insufficient amount of oxygen, respiration will cease, and you will die. Luckily, the atmosphere is a relatively stable feature of the environment, there is likely to be plenty of oxygen for some time to come. However, environments can become volatile, and the human creature is in many respects frail. As environments are dynamic compounds of interacting forces, they can become unstable. Tornadoes, floods, plagues, drought, wildfires, and earthquakes are obvious examples of how an environment can threaten human safety. In such instances, the organism must enlist the support of other factors within the environment to help address the difficulty, as when water is used to extinguish fire and antibiotics are used to combat disease.

We need not turn to large-scale cases of catastrophe for examples of how an environment can grow unstable and hence problematic. Instability exists at more local levels as well. Sunburn, frostbite, and dehydration are familiar hazards. These occur when the interaction of the human organism with certain features of the environment is strained, hindered, or obstructed; the environment poses a challenge that the organism cannot meet. Damage to the organism results. If the damage is extreme, the organism dies. Additionally, we may of course cite less dramatic cases. The breeze blowing through my study carried my notes to the floor, thereby creating a disturbance; in recovering them I attempt to restore order to the environment. The light from the Sun creates a glare on my computer screen such that I cannot read the words I'm typing. I respond by drawing the blinds. That is, I *intervene* with current conditions, I use the environment to *alter* the environment; in a minor way, I change the world.

Perhaps we are now able to understand the quotation with which the chapter began. Living involves a gamble because life depends upon interaction within an environment that is prone to instability. Even the instability of the environment is uncertain—the instabilities are unstable! The dangers of the environment are "irregular, inconstant, not to be counted upon as to their times and seasons" (*EN*, LW1:43). Conversely, environments are episodically stable. The world is not a total chaos, not everything changes all at once. Although nothing is ultimately immutable, certain factors in the environment are for the most part regular. We conclude, with Dewey, that the world is both precarious *and* stable, hence its aleatory, risky character.

Human creatures thus find themselves in a difficult predicament. Despite the perilous nature of the environment and all the attendant risks and insecurities, they must nonetheless *act*:

> At every moment, the living creature is exposed to dangers from its surroundings, and at every moment, it must draw upon something in its surroundings to satisfy its needs. The career and destiny of a living being are bound up with the its interchanges with its environment, not externally, but in the most intimate way. (*AE*, LW10:19)

The environment *calls for* action, it *requires* a response. If we do not act or if we act inappropriately, we shall suffer adverse consequences and perhaps die. And yet, any action one undertakes is itself a potential source of future uncertainty. There is no guarantee in advance that a particular course of action will sufficiently respond to the environment. Moreover, in acting one introduces changes into the present environment, but there is never absolute assurance that those changes will be to one's benefit. Some actions will not meet the challenges of current conditions. Others may be sufficient to meet present dangers, but will generate other, more hazardous conditions in the future. Although necessary, action is risky.

What has this to do with philosophy? People often think of philosophy as aloof, detached thinking. Dewey takes a different view:

> It is submitted that just this predicament of the inextricable mixture of stability and uncertainty gives rise to philosophy, and that it is reflected in all its recurrent problems and issues. (*EN*, LW1:46)

Dewey maintains philosophy arises in response to the plight of the live creature in an aleatory world. This is a bold claim. To see that it is true we shall have to fill in a bit more of Dewey's account.

The Response: Escaping from Peril

Perpetual confrontation with the precarious takes its toll on the live creature; if it is to survive, it must develop techniques that respond to perilous conditions. That is, the live creature must attempt to *control* its environment. Dewey argues that the human creature has devised two general strategies for control within an aleatory world. In general terms, these strategies take the form of supplication and tradition on the one hand, and science and technology on the other.

The earliest humans sought control through supplication. As they lacked tools and other means of protection and power, they were literally at the mercy of their environment. They imagined that their surroundings were under the direction of hidden forces and supernatural entities that could be contacted and influenced through ritual and sacrifice. This strategy is manifest in the myths, rites, and superstitions of our distant ancestors. For them, environmental crises such as failed crops, floods, and disease were indications of displeased spirits. It was thought that through ritual one could appease offended deities and restore order. According to this technique, security is gained by adopting the correct emotional and spiritual stance towards the supernatural forces which govern the world and hence control fate.

Over time, the methods of supplication become systematized and socially generalized. "A certain texture of tradition is built up," there arises a "communal way of conceiving life"; quasi-religious myths and rites become the defining feature of a clan, band, tribe, or nation (*RP*, MW12:84). This is to say that *culture* arises around the practices and superstitions associated with supplication. The development of a culture signals the formulation of habits, customs, institutions, social rules, and official doctrines regarding behavior. Most generally, a culture is marked by a *moral* tradition, a picture of our place in the universe, a vision of the *meaning* and significance of human life.

The strategy of supplication, of turning inward to win the favor of controlling forces, is ultimately unreliable. Dangers can befall the purest heart, hazards persist despite the greatest hope. Furthermore, as "the requirements of continued existence make indispensable some attention to the actual facts of the world" (*RP*, MW12:85), the methods of supplication cannot be universally applied. A second tactic for dealing with the vicissitudes of life thus develops. This strategy involves turning "the powers of nature to account" by "changing the world through action" (*QC*, LW4:3). The direct *confrontation* with hostile surroundings gives rise to practical arts associated with tool-making, agriculture, and hunting. By such means, humans learn to *transform* conditions to better suit their needs. It is through action upon the environment, and not the alteration of inner attitudes, that the live creature gains control. As the techniques of transformation become more sophisticated, the degree of control increases.

Along with increased control, there arises a stock of common-sense beliefs about the world: wood burns, sharp points cut, fire is hot, heavy objects fall, animals can be trapped, some plants are poisonous. "Gradually there grows up a body of homely generalizations" about the "observed facts and sequences of nature." Yet the techniques of transformation "provide not merely a collection of positive facts," they also "give expertness of dealing with materials and tools, and promote the development of the experimental habit of mind" (*RP*, MW12:85-86). Eventually, science and technology are born.

The history of the human creature is bound up with the tandem careers of these two modes of response. The scientific mode produces practical arts and technologies that in turn give rise to a system of matter-of-fact knowledge about the world. The supplicatory mode generates a cultural tradition of custom, religion, and morality. As long as scientific thinking is relatively unsystematic and isolated, non-scientific culture may happily co-exist with science. However, scientific thinking has a cumulative effect. "As the arts and crafts develop and become more elaborate, the body of positive and tested knowledge enlarges. . ." (*RP*, MW12:86). As scientific knowledge expands, the potential for conflict with traditional beliefs and values increases.

History provides many examples of how science can come into direct conflict with traditional beliefs. Consider the case of Galileo in the seventeenth century. The prevailing thesis prior to Galileo was that the motionless Earth was at the center of the universe and hence that all other heavenly objects revolved around it. A body of religious and moral doctrines had been built around this view. It was thought that because the Earth occupied a central position in the universe, humans occupied a central position in the attention of the creator of the universe. Galileo was able to show that the *geocentric* ("Earth-centered") conception of the universe was incorrect, and that the evidence supported the *heliocentric* ("Sun-centered") model of the universe first proposed by Copernicus. This advance in astronomy undermined the traditional culture. Humans could no longer appeal to the structure of the universe to support claims to self-importance; the Earth was just one among many bodies revolving around the Sun. As we know, Galileo was arrested and punished by the dominant cultural institution of his day. We find contemporary and thankfully less extreme examples of the clash of tradition with science in disputes regarding technological interventions with human life: euthanasia, cloning, genetic engineering, and artificial intelligence.

The live creature's efforts to escape from peril generate two distinct products: tradition and science. As these modes of response grow from different sources, there arises a new *kind* of difficulty with which humans must deal, namely, that of reconciling the morals and customs of tradition with the methods, knowledge, and attitudes of science. Dewey submits that, "the origin of philosophy lay in an attempt to reconcile the two different types of mental product" (*RP*, MW12:89). Hence Dewey's fundamental metaphilosophical postulate:

> . . . the distinctive office, problems, and subjectmatter of philosophy grow out of the stresses and strains in the community life in which a given form of philosophy arises. . . its specific problems vary with the changes in human life that are always going on and that at times constitute a crisis and a turning point in human history. (*RP*, MW12:256)

The ancient Greek philosopher, Plato, famously declared that philosophy begins with "wonder."[4] Dewey has argued that philosophy arises out of a particular set of social conditions. Philosophy thus does not "develop in an unbiased way from an open and unprejudiced origin," rather, it has "a task cut out for it from the start"(*RP*, MW12:89). Philosophy has a *social* mission.

Dewey's Analysis of the Philosophical Tradition

The Rise of Philosophy: Searching for the Immutable

The initial response to the clash of tradition with science was to introduce a *social* distinction through which the conflicting factors may be separated. Those who practiced the arts and crafts associated with science were historically relegated to a social class of "common" artisans, craftsmen, and laborers. The "noble" and ruling classes, by contrast, took no part in the productive arts; rather, they maintained the traditional culture through detachment from worldly affairs.

However, this kind of response could not succeed for long. The time came when scientific knowledge grew to such an extent that the conflict could no longer be contained by class divisions. In light of the success of the scientific approach in confronting the world's perils, traditional beliefs could no longer claim authority in the world of everyday experience. Hence there was a need to, "Develop a method of rational investigation . . . which should place the essential elements of traditional belief upon an unshakable basis" (*RP*, MW12:89).

Whereas traditional beliefs had previously relied upon the force of habit and custom for justification, now there was needed a more permanent foundation. As such a foundation could not be found within the natural world which science was mastering, the foundation needed to be supernatural, metaphysical, and therefore beyond the reach of scientific investigation; "that which had rested upon custom was to be restored, resting no longer upon the habits of the past, but upon the very metaphysics of Being and the Universe" (*RP*, MW12:89).

Philosophy thus undertook to "justify on rational grounds the spirit. . . of accepted beliefs and traditional customs." The initial move in this attempt was to introduce a "fixed and fundamental distinction between two realms of existence" (*RP*, MW12:90-92). Traditional philosophies thus typically feature what we may call the 'two worlds' theory of reality. The philosophy of Plato is a compelling example of this tendency.[5] Plato famously noted that the spatio-temporal world which we encounter in ordinary experience is a world of change and decay. Such a world, Plato argued, is therefore corrupt and ultimately unintelligible; since the world we experience is constantly in a state of change, of *becoming* something new, it is not possible to have knowledge of what it *is*. He thus contrived a non-spatio-temporal realm, the "World of Ideas," which was populated not by the objects of experience but by abstract entities he called "Forms." On Plato's view, Forms are eternal, ideal, unchanging, and perfect; they are apprehended not by the bodily organs of sense-experience, but by "Reason," a special power of the soul. True knowledge was gained only through withdrawal from the world of physical existence and experience; through philosophy—the exercise of Reason—one came in contact with the Forms and acquired real knowledge.

Hence, on the Platonic view, the knowledge associated with the scientific study of the world was depreciated. As science concerns itself with a metaphysically corrupt world of change, its products—the beliefs, attitudes, and methods that are its outcome—are epistemologically inferior to those of philosophical reflection. The earlier class division employed to contain science is thus translated by philosophy into a *metaphysical dualism*, an opposition between different *kinds* of existence. According to Plato, there is an essential metaphysical opposition between the physical world and the ideal world of Forms. This dualism further generates an *epistemological dualism*, an opposition between different kinds of knowledge. Whereas the sensory experience connects one to the illusory world of physical objects and hence cannot generate real knowledge, the mental faculty of Reason apprehends the ideal Forms, the true objects of knowledge. With experience, and thus science, relegated to a subordinate realm of being, traditional values and customs—represented by the 'higher' reality with which philosophy deals—are preserved and protected.

The tendency to preserve tradition through the introduction of dualism is not peculiar to Platonism. Traditional philosophies of the most diverse stripes have employed this tactic in one way or another. We find in Aristotle a dualism of Form and Matter, in St. Augustine a dualism of the City of God and the City of Man, in Descartes a dualism of Mind and Body, and in Kant a dualism of Noumena and Phenomena. In each case, the first term of the dualism refers to an eternal and immutable kind of existence which is the source and object of true knowledge and "which could be apprehended only by the systematic discipline of philosophy." The remaining term invariably denotes the "ordinary empirical, relatively real, phenomenal world of everyday experience," the "imperfect and perishing world" that is the concern of science (*RP*, MW12:92). Hence, "Philosophy is marked,"

> . . . by a division of its subject-matter into the truly real and the merely apparent, a subject and an object, a physical and a mental, and ideal and an actual, that have nothing to do with one another, save in some mode which is so mysterious as to create an insoluble problem. (*QC*, LW4:195)

Taking itself to be the dispassionate and uncompromising pursuit of Truth, traditional philosophy placed itself above the affairs of everyday life and above the practices of science. Dewey writes:

> Philosophy has arrogated to itself the office of demonstrating the existence of a transcendent, absolute or inner reality and of revealing to man the nature and features of this higher reality. It has therefore claimed that it was in possession of a higher organ of knowledge than is employed by positive science and ordinary practical experience, and that it is marked by a superior dignity . . . . (*RP*, MW12:92)

And so,

> Philosophical doctrines which disagreed about virtually everything else were at one in the assumption that their distinctive concern as philosophy was to search for the immutable and ultimate—that which *is*—without respect to the temporal or spacial. (*RP*, MW12:260)

Historically, philosophy has taken itself to be a discipline which, because it studies a "higher" kind of reality, somehow stands above the concerns of everyday life and the practices of other disciplines.[6]

Dewey's Critique of the Tradition

Of course, Dewey's analysis of the origins of philosophical dualism does not constitute an objection to the philosophical practice of drawing distinctions. Rather, Dewey objects to the practice of translating intellectual *distinctions* into supposedly fixed and eternal *dualisms*. Once introduced, dualisms generate the problem of how the separated entities could be related. Consider Plato—once the dualism of the physical world and the World of Ideas was introduced, he then had the hopeless problem of how these two worlds were related to each other. This is a problem that, as Aristotle argued, Plato was never able to sufficiently resolve.[7]

Dewey argues that the dualisms of traditional philosophy do not capture fixed and eternal disjunctions in reality, but rather arise out of specific social conditions. As such they are unfit for dealing with current difficulties. Moreover, as traditional dualisms are the source of the strictly intellectual problem of uniting what they have driven asunder, a philosophy which maintains them encourages and promotes another unfortunate trend in the history of philosophy: apathetic detachment, other-worldliness, estrangement, complacency.

Because philosophers have traditionally taken themselves to be concerned with ultimate truths of the sort that could be found only in a transcendent, changeless realm, they have withdrawn from the world. Fixing their attention upon a supposedly superior realm, they have abandoned ordinary life, rendering philosophy irrelevant. Convinced that they alone have been pursuing Truth, philosophers have come to comprise an elite intellectual class of thinkers who work on exotic and unusual problems—more correctly, they are "puzzles" (*EN*, LW1:17)—in isolation from every other intellectual endeavor.

Even today there persists the idea that there are special "problems" which it is the distinctive job of philosophers to address. Typically, such problems are completely divorced from everyday life. Furthermore, philosophy is conducted in a specialized, technical vocabulary addressed to a catalogue of esoteric issues. As only philosophers know this vocabulary and the corresponding issues, it is almost impossible for those outside the professional academic discipline to know what philosophers do. It is hard to resist the conclusion that philosophy is a means of escape from the world in which we must live. Characterizing philosophy's prevalent attitudes towards the world of everyday experience, Dewey writes:

> The creeds that have prevailed have been founded upon the supposed necessity of escape from the confusion and uncertainties of experience. Life has been thought to be evil and hopeless unless it could be shown to bear within itself the assured promise of a higher reality. Philosophies of escape have also been philosophies of compensation for the ills and sufferings of the experienced world. (LW5:268)[8]

However, Dewey maintains that whereas philosophers have "seen themselves, and represented themselves to the public, as dealing with something which has variously been termed Being, Nature or the

Universe, the cosmos at large, Reality, or Truth" (*RP*, MW12:260), they have actually, though perhaps unwittingly, been "occupied with the precious values embedded in social traditions" (*RP*, MW12:94). Without realizing it, philosophers have been performing a social function, namely, that of protecting the customs associated with traditional culture from the threat of scientific examination. As these traditions are the products of the pre-scientific and anti-scientific tendencies of primitive myth, cult, and superstition, it is unclear that they have a legitimate claim to authority in present affairs.

"Philosophy must take, with good grace, its own medicine" (MW10:38).[9] That is, philosophy must subject its own methods, assumptions, and principles to rigorous analysis and criticism. With this done, it will be seen that, "what philosophy has been unconsciously, without knowing it or intending it, and, so to speak, under cover, it must henceforth be openly and deliberately." Just as traditional philosophies arose out of the social need to reconcile culture with science, "the task of future philosophy is to clarify men's ideas as to the social and moral strifes of their own day" (*RP*, MW12:94). Therefore, philosophers must abandon the puzzles they have inherited from the tradition, and turn their attention to problems facing society. Reconstructed philosophy thus becomes a mode of social criticism, an instrument of social reform.[10] Put most generally, philosophy must "recover" its social mission. Dewey writes:

> Philosophy recovers itself when it ceases to be a device for dealing with the problems of philosophers and becomes a method, cultivated by philosophers, for dealing with the problems of men. (MW10:46)

From his insistence that philosophy return to the concerns of the world, Dewey derives "a first-rate test of the value of any philosophy which is offered us":

> Does it end in conclusions which, when they are referred back to ordinary life-experiences and their predicaments, render them more significant, more luminous to us, and make our dealings with them more fruitful? Or does it terminate in rendering the things of ordinary experience more opaque then they were before, and in depriving them of having in "reality" even the significance they had previously seemed to have? (*EN*, LW1:18)

Like traditional philosophies, a reconstructed philosophy must perform the decisive social function of reconciling culture and science. However, unlike the traditional approach, which unconsciously aimed to protect tradition from science by means of dualism, reconstructed philosophy must be directed to the *integration* of science and culture. Reconstructed philosophy must strive to apply the methods of science to the moral and social problems facing contemporary culture.

The General Strategy for Reconstruction

Certainly, it is not enough merely to state that philosophers should abandon certain aspects of their tradition and turn their attention to problems facing contemporary society. The practices, attitudes, and methods of traditional ways of thinking are well embedded in the practice of contemporary philosophers. As such, the principles underlying philosophy cannot be directly refuted; they are "more than abstract logical forms and categories," they are "habits, predispositions, deeply engrained attitudes of aversion and preference" (MW4:14).[11] The effort to reconstruct philosophy therefore must begin by taking a *genetic* approach to traditional philosophy. That is, the *sources* of the traditional problems must be attacked. One must demonstrate that the traditional problems arise *only if* we adopt a certain vocabulary and certain presuppositions which we have good reason to reject. As Dewey puts it, "we do not solve" the problems of traditional philosophy, "we get over them" (MW4:14).

At the core of Dewey's approach is a view regarding the implications of Darwinism for philosophy. Dewey writes:

> In laying hands upon the sacred ark of absolute permanency, in treating the forms that had been regarded as types of fixity and perfection as originating and passing away, the *Origin of Species* introduced a mode of thinking that in the end was bound to transform the logic of knowledge, and hence the treatment of morals, politics, and religion. (MW4:3)

Darwin's lesson is that *process*, not immutability, is the primary feature of reality. By showing that traditional philosophy's search for the immutable is futile; Darwin has set the program for reconstruction. In coming chapters, we will find Dewey arguing that the leading problems of traditional philosophy are cast in the archaic conceptual vocabulary of a pre-Darwinian world-view. His strategy is not to respond directly to these problems, but rather to *challenge* them *as* problems, to show that *as* problems they are obsolete and ought to be abandoned. It is in this sense that reconstructed philosophy "gets over" traditional puzzles; "Old questions are solved by disappearing, evaporating, while new questions corresponding to the changed attitude of endeavor and preference take their place" (MW4:14).

A reconstructed philosophy does not pretend to somehow stand above the natural sciences; rather philosophy must *begin* with science. Again, the task of a reconstructed philosophy is to apply the methods of scientific investigation to social problems, "its aim is to become so far as is humanly possible, an instrument for dealing with these conflicts" (MW12:94). A reconstructed philosophy is *scientific*.

Summary

We live in an aleatory world. Survival depends upon our ability to control our surroundings. Humans have developed two strategies for gaining control. One strategy advocates supplication as a means of influencing supernatural forces which supposedly govern the world; it gives rise to myth and ritual. This method marks the origin of culture and morality. A second strategy attempts to gain control through action upon the environment. This tactic marks the birth of science.

The practice of scientific methods generates a body of empirical beliefs about the world. As this body of empirical knowledge increases, it challenges the traditional beliefs generated and perpetuated by culture. Philosophy is the attempt to reconcile such conflict. Therefore, philosophy is not a neutral search for the truth, it is the product of the social conditions of specific times and places.

Traditional philosophies have sought to resolve the conflict of tradition with science through the introduction of dualisms by which the values and principles associated with the dominant culture were elevated to a realm of superior reality. Accordingly, scientific methods and the world of common experience with which science deals are relegated to a realm of lesser reality and inferior metaphysical status. Traditional philosophies have therefore been directed towards protecting cultural values from scientific examination.

Reconstructed philosophy reverses the picture. On Dewey's view, philosophy must appropriate scientific methods in dealing with the "problems of men." Such a philosophy would abandon the inherited puzzles and turn its attention to social criticism. Thus, philosophy would cease to be a special discipline with its own problems and specialized vocabulary practiced by a detached class of intellectuals; reconstructed philosophy is necessarily *public* philosophy.

Before a reconstructed philosophy can emerge, traditional ways of philosophizing must be rehabilitated. Dewey adopts a genetic approach to reconstructing current philosophy; that is, Dewey attacks the source of philosophical problems. He attempts to demonstrate that the traditional problems of philosophy arise out of premises associated with a pre-Darwinian view of the world. With these premises abandoned, the stage is set for a new *kind* of philosophy based upon Darwinian principles.

Endnotes

[1] *A Pluralistic Universe* (Cambridge: Harvard, 1977), 14.
[2] The prefix 'meta' is a Greek word which literally means 'after' but has come to have the connotation of 'beyond' or 'above'. Thus, 'metaphilosophy' is philosophy that stands 'above' philosophy itself; that is, philosophical thinking about philosophy.
[3] See *Art As Experience* (*AE*, LW10:18ff).
[4] Plato, *Theaetetus* (155d). Compare Dewey, "Classic philosophy was conceived in wonder, born in leisure and bred in consummatory contemplation" (*EN*, LW1:101).
[5] See Plato's *Phaedo* and *Republic* for a 'two worlds' metaphysics.
[6] Consider that the name of the highest academic degree in America is the "Doctor of Philosophy" (Ph. D.). The suggestion seems to be that once one understands the *philosophical* dimension of a subject, one has learned all that another person can teach.
[7] See especially Aristotle, *Metaphysics* Book A, 991a9ff.
[8] "What I Believe" (LW5:267-278).
[9] "The Need for a Recovery of Philosophy" (MW10:3-48).
[10] The view the philosophy must become a vehicle of social criticism is expressed in *Experience and Nature* (*EN*, LW1:304-308).
[11] "The Influence of Darwinism on Philosophy" (MW4:3-14).

3
Reconstructing Experience

Issues in *epistemology*[1] have dominated philosophy's Modern period.[2] Specifically, philosophers have sought to understand the relation of experience to knowledge. Without too much risk of oversimplification, one can read the history of Modern philosophy as a contest between two attitudes about the epistemological value of experience. 'Rationalists' maintain that experience is the source of illusion and error, and therefore is an obstacle to knowledge. Rene Descartes (1596-1650), a rationalist who is often called the "father of Modern philosophy," argued that experience is systematically deceptive. He is perhaps most famous for his argument that, on the basis of experience, one could never determine whether one is dreaming or awake![3] Rationalists therefore have sought to locate the source of knowledge entirely within the mind's faculty of Reason.

'Empiricists' are suspicious of the rationalists' appeal to Reason. Arguing that Reason is an abstract faculty bearing no connection to the physical world, empiricists maintain that Reason could supply only the most trivial kind of knowledge. To employ a common example, one can know by Reason that 'all bachelors are unmarried'. Empiricists argue that this so-called knowledge consists in simply apprehending the *definitions* of the terms employed; Reason can supply the knowledge that 'all bachelors are unmarried' simply because 'bachelor' *means* 'unmarried person'. This supposed knowledge is vacuous; it rests upon how we use words and says nothing about what is the case in the world. Reason cannot tell me, for example, whether some particular person, P, is a bachelor or not.

Insisting that we should reserve the appellation 'knowledge' for that which puts us in touch with the world rather than the meanings of our terms, empiricists have sought to construct a theory of knowledge based upon experience. According to empiricism, experience alone provides the necessary connection between the mind and the world, and is therefore the source of all knowledge. In the words of John Locke (1632-1704), the leading exponent of Modern empiricism,

> Let us then suppose the Mind to be, as we say, white Paper, void of all Characters, without any *Ideas*; How come it to be furnished? [. . .] To this I answer, in one word, *Experience*: In that, all our Knowledge is founded; and from that it ultimately derives it self.[4]

Dewey is a kind of empiricist. Like the Modern empiricist, whom we shall call the "traditional empiricist," Dewey maintains that experience is the source of knowledge; however, he rejects the traditional empiricists' view of what experience is. Dewey *reconstructs* the Modern conception of experience; he promotes a reconstructed variety of empiricism which, for reasons that shall become clear later, we may call 'radical empiricism'. As Dewey's conception of experience is best appreciated when seen in contrast to the traditional theory, we begin with the traditional conception of experience.

The decision to examine the concept of experience at this point in our study is not capricious. In his essay, "The Need for a Recovery of Philosophy," Dewey insists that,

> . . . it is just the inherited view of experience common to the empirical school and its opponents which keeps alive many discussions even of matters that on their face are quite remote from it, while it is also this view which is most untenable in the light of existing science and social practice. (MW10:5)

As we shall discover in the course of our analysis, the conception of experience operative in traditional empiricism generates many of the infamous philosophical "puzzles" which, as we saw in the last chapter, Dewey wants philosophers to abandon. The effort to reconstruct philosophy must therefore begin with an analysis of this theory of experience. Once the traditional view has been undermined, a new view of experience—a new empiricism—can be developed in its place.

The Traditional Theory of Experience

Constructing the Traditional Theory

"To know the meaning of empiricism, we need to understand what experience is" (*EE*, LW13:11). The claim that knowledge comes through experience is uninformative unless we are told what experience is. What is experience? Philosophers have offered what may seem a plausible answer, namely, that experience is sensory perception. Having an experience is a matter of perceiving an object with one's senses. I am now looking at the apple that sits nearby; I see an apple-shaped patch of deep red against the background of the books, papers, and other objects that are positioned on my desk. When I move my head in even the slightest way, my experience alters accordingly, revealing to my vision the three-dimensional aspect of the apple. I place my hand on the apple and inspect its texture. I am now having a tactile experience; I feel a smooth, curved surface. As I lift the apple and bring it to my mouth, I can smell the apple. When I bite, I hear the distinctive crunch of an apple being bitten and then I taste the sweetness unique to apples. I have now had a series of experiences: visual, tactile, olfactory, auditory, and finally, gustatory.

This conception of experience may seem so plainly evident that it hardly deserves to be called a "theory." Nevertheless, beneath this seemingly innocent conception there lies a swarm of difficulties that require extensive philosophical treatment. To see these difficulties, consider familiar cases of perceptual error. Place half of a straight stick into a swimming pool. What do you see? The stick will appear to bend at the water's surface. Now stand at one end of a long corridor. Do the walls appear to converge in the distance? Perhaps you have had the experience of driving on a straight road on a hot summer's day. Often, one will perceive a puddle of water on the road in the distance which mysteriously disappears once approached. Additionally, consider the special set of perceptual errors called "optical illusions." You're probably familiar with the Necker box, a two-dimensional drawing that appears to be a three-dimensional cube. 3-D computer games provide another convenient example.

What these considerations have suggested to philosophers is that sensory perception is *representational*. That is, sense experience does not provide a direct connection to the world; rather, it plays the mediatory role of providing an *image* of the world. Were this not the case, were sense experience a *direct* connection to the world, it would be impossible to account for perceptual error. Denying that sense experience is representational would require one to make absurd assertions such as that sticks *actually do bend* in water.

What seemed a simple conception of experience is now becoming philosophically complex; it may help to introduce some technical vocabulary. Once we accept that experience is representational, we must distinguish the *representation* from the *object* represented. When I look at the apple on my desk, I am presented with a certain *image*, it is a representation of a certain physical *object*, namely, the apple. The *object*, the apple, sits on my desk. It bears certain relations to other objects, such as the desk upon which it sits. The apple is also next to my watch, below the ceiling, and in front of my books; it is heavier than my watch and lighter than my desk; it is taller than a dime but shorter than I am. These are mundane observations; now let us ask some philosophical questions. Where does the *representation*, the *image* of the apple, reside? In what does this image consist? How is it produced?

It may seem that the representation resides inside my skull, perhaps somewhere behind my eyes. Is this plausible? I am now looking at my apple again. Suppose you were to look inside my skull as I looked at my apple, what would you see? Would you see an image of an apple? No; you would probably see a brain, blood vessels, and cerebrospinal fluid. Maybe you would then look inside my brain. Is the image of an apple inside my brain? No; inside my brain there are neurons, more blood vessels, and more cerebrospinal fluid. Where, then, is the representation of the apple? Again, what at first seemed a simple answer has proven to contain some complications!

Let's review. We began with the idea that experience is sense perception. We then took note of the existence of perceptual error. Wanting to avoid conclusions such as "straight sticks bend whenever they are placed in water," we decided that sense perception does not provide *direct* access to the world, but rather involves representation.

Hence, we say that the stick *appears* bent in the water, recognizing that the actual stick is nevertheless straight. We then distinguished the representation from the object represented. We considered a particular object, the apple, and discovered that we could locate this object in relation to other objects. We then discovered that we could not easily do the same with the representation of the apple, and we got stuck. The question remains, Where is the representation of the apple?

Some philosophers have suggested that it is mistake to think that we should be able to locate the representation of the apple as we can locate the apple itself. They have argued that whereas the object is physical and therefore locatable within space, the representation is not physical, does not exist in space, and thus cannot be "found" by observation. The representation of the apple, they continue, exists in the *mind* of the person perceiving the apple; apples exist in the physical realm, but apple representations exist in a separate realm of minds. Unlike the apple representation, which is known directly through a special mental faculty known as 'introspection', the apple is known indirectly through the awareness of the apple representation.

Here, then, lies the core of the traditional theory of experience. It is a sophisticated theory which has been very popular in the history of philosophy. It is important to reckon its leading features. Firstly, we note that this theory transfers a distinction we made between the representation and the object represented into a metaphysical dualism. The object, the apple, belongs to an order of existence that is different from that to which the representation, the image of the apple, belongs; the apple is *physical* whereas the representation is *mental*. We see also that this initial dualism is generalized into a further dualism between a physical, "external" world inhabited by physical bodies such as apples and a non-physical, "internal" world of minds and mental images. Lastly, there is an epistemological dualism between the apple, which is known indirectly through sense experience, and the representation of the apple, which is known directly through introspection.

We now find ourselves in a predicament. Our theory claims that there are minds that contain mental representations and there is a physical world that contains physical objects. However, it is clear that these supposedly separate realms must be related, for it seems that, unless I'm dreaming or hallucinating, the apple representation occurs only when the object, the apple, is present. Put another way, it seems that "internal" apple representations are usually *caused* by "external" apples. The theory thus requires some means of establishing this causal relation between physical objects of the external world and the mental representations they generate in the internal realm.

We therefore must admit an intermediary kind of entity into our theory which can bridge the gap between the inner world of mental representation and the outer world of physical objects. Traditional empiricists have adopted various terms to describe this third term; John Locke speaks of physical objects emitting "imperceptible bodies" which produce "motion" in the brain and thereby generate "ideas" in the mind.[5] Updating Locke, we may speak of 'sense data' instead of "imperceptible bodies." Sense data are insensible bits of information which are emitted from physical objects and causally interact with the sensory organs of a suitably positioned observer to produce a series of events within the observer's central nervous system; the events in the nervous system in turn generate a mental representation, an "idea." Returning to our apple example, the apple emits a certain set of sense data containing information about the apple. In the case of visual experience, the data causally affect my eyes and stimulate the optic nerve. The stimulation of the optic nerve causes a part of my brain called the visual cortex to be stimulated, and this in turn generates a particular mental image—the deep red of a ripe apple.

Similar accounts can be given for the other modes of sensory experience. Consider a case involving audition. I strike a key on a piano. This causes a string within the piano to vibrate. The vibration of the string then causes a certain kind of disturbance in the air which we call a 'sound wave'—we could just as easily say that the string emits a certain sense datum about its vibration. The data come in contact with my ear, and stimulate my auditory nerve. This stimulation in turn causes a certain part of my brain to be stimulated, and this brain activity generates an auditory image in my mind of the pitch we call 'D'. Through the introduction of an intermediary entity, then, it seems we have explained the nature of the representational character of experience and thereby arrived at a plausible theory of experience.

Troubles with the Traditional Theory

Although the theory of experience just sketched may appear satisfactory, it is the source of difficult problems. In the first place, one might wonder whether we have been begging important questions by using the term 'representation' to describe the mental images present in experience. The term 'representation' might be question-begging because it implies that there is a *correspondence* between the mental image and the object that causes it. That is, we have thus far assumed that, via sense data, the apple on my desk causes a mental image of deep red which *corresponds* to, "represents," the actual color of the apple. What reason do we have to accept this? How could such a claim be verified? To establish that the red I see when I look at the apple actually represents the color of the apple, I would have to be able to *compare* the mental image with the apple. On our theory, such comparison is impossible; my only access to the apple is through the images provided by sense experience. That is, I can never get outside my sensory perception to compare the apple to my mental image of the apple. As the German philosopher, Immanuel Kant (1724-1804) would say, I can never know the apple as it exists "in itself."[6]

Think of it this way.[7] Suppose you are watching a television program about the Parthenon in Greece, wondering whether it is actually as majestic as it appears on the screen. You might take a trip to Greece to compare the picture on the television with the real thing. However, suppose you are unable to travel to Greece and can only encounter the Parthenon by means of television. Could you establish that the television image of the Parthenon *accurately* represents the actual Parthenon? You could not. On our theory, what we directly encounter in experience is a mental image, we have no direct access to the objects which cause the images. It thus seems that our theory does not have the necessary resources to justify the assumption that mental images are true representations of external objects.

This consideration has led philosophers to avoid the term 'representation' and adopt more neutral terms to refer to the mental images presented in sense experience. Locke employs the term 'idea'; others, such as Bertrand Russell, have adopted the term 'sensation'. To avoid confusing the many senses of 'idea', we shall adopt Russell's term. We may say that objects emit sense data which in turn cause sensations in the mind; however, the relation of sensations to the objects that cause them remains a mystery.

A second problem arises out of the first. Once it is realized that our theory cannot establish that our experiences actually represent external objects, the door is opened to a more sweeping objection. What reason do we have to believe in an "external world" of objects at all? The Irish philosopher George Berkeley (1685-1753), argued on traditional empiricist grounds that no physical objects exist.[8] His argument is that since we encounter only sensations in experience, we have no reason to believe that there is anything *beyond* them. Put another way, if empiricism is the view that all knowledge comes from experience, and if experience is always *mental*, then the empiricist has no reason to believe in a physical world. Therefore the common sense belief that when I see an apple it is because there *is* a certain physical object out in the world *causing* me to see an apple is, on Berkeley's view, unjustified. Accordingly, Berkeley argues that empiricism leads to *idealism*, the view that only minds and ideas exist.

One might respond to the idealist in the following manner. Although one cannot claim to *know* that one's experiences are caused by physical objects, there is still reason to *believe* that there are such objects. The empiricist is justified in believing in objects, the response continues, because the assumption that objects exist and cause our experiences provides the best explanation of the *continuities* and *regularities* within experience. Whenever I look at the apple, I see deep red; whenever I strike this key on my piano, I hear a 'D'. Moreover, when I close my eyes, the image of the apple disappears and reappears only once I open my eyes. Why should there be these stable patterns in experience?

Consider further the cases of perceptual error. If there is nothing beyond my immediate experience, why should we call such events "errors"? Suppose a friend looking at a stick half submerged in water were to declare, "That stick is bent." Doesn't the fact that we should like to say that our friend has made a mistake suggest that there *is* a stick that exists independently of anyone's experience of it and that this stick is straight? Unless we assume that there are objects that are independent of our ideas, we shall not be able to explain our most basic intuitions. The belief in physical objects is therefore justified.

Through an appeal to the regular features of experience, we seem to have saved the common sense belief in the existence of an external world of ordinary physical objects. However, this defense gives rise to a third difficulty commonly associated with David Hume.[9] How do we know that there are regularities in our experience? Do we experience *regularities*? What is the source of our belief in such stabilities?

These questions may sound silly. However, there is a serious difficulty underlying our appeal to the regularity of experience. To see this, it is necessary to acknowledge a feature of the traditional view of experience that we have not yet considered. According to the traditional view, a sensation is the product of the impact of discrete and particular sense data on one's sensory organs. As sense data cause sensations, and each datum is discrete and particular, each sensation is discrete and particular. That is, experience is arranged much like the frames on a film-strip; each sensation is like a single frame.

Let's conduct an experiment. The time is now 12:30 (call this "time 1," "t1" for short), and I am looking at my apple. I see an apple-shaped patch of deep red (call this "sensation 1," "s1" for short). We can thus say that at t1 I am presented with s1. The time is now 12:31 (t2); I close my eyes and see blackness (s2). I reopen my eyes a few seconds later (t3) and am presented with an apple-shaped patch of deep red (s3). Common sense tells me that s1 is in some way identical to s3. Of course, s1 and s3 cannot be strictly identical since they occurred at different times. Philosophers use the term 'qualitative identity' to denote the sense in which s1 and s3 seem to be the same. To say that s1 and s3 are qualitatively identical is to say that the deep red of s1 is the *same* deep red, has the same *quality*, as that presented in s3. How can this be established?

It is now t4, and I am comparing in memory s1 and s3. According to my memory, s1 and s3 were qualitatively identical. Is this sufficient to establish the qualitative identity of s1 and s3, and thereby establish that there is continuity in experience? Perhaps not; memory does not provide direct access to s1 and s3—my memory of s1 and s3 occurs at t4 whereas s1 occurred at t1 and s3 occurred at t3. What reason do I have to believe that my memory is reliable? Can the reliability of my memories of s1 and s3 be established? No; my memories of s1 and s3 are themselves sensations, and so the problem of establishing the accuracy of my memory is really just another case of trying to establish the representative accuracy of my sensations. As we saw earlier, one cannot on the basis of sensations establish that they are accurate representations of external objects. Now we find that one cannot establish on the basis of sensations in memory that they are accurate representations of past sensations. The problem is intractable.

We have been through some of the thorniest philosophical territory, so let's review. Once it is conceded that there is no way for the traditional empiricist to establish that inner sensations are accurate representations of outer objects, the stage is set for the idealist to deny the existence of an external world. Wanting to avoid this, we appealed to the fact that there are certain regularities and continuities within experience which are best explained by the thesis that there *are* objects which exist outside of the mind and which cause ideas to occur within the mind. Then we conducted an experiment which challenged our confidence in these regularities. The experiment demonstrated that just as we cannot justify through experience the belief that sensations are accurate representations of external objects, we cannot justify through experience the belief that there are regularities in experience. Our response to the idealist has failed; the traditional view of experience forces us to reject the belief in the existence of an external world.

The traditional conception of experience with which we began leads to a series of tough philosophical problems. These problems, along with several others which we have not considered, have led some traditional empiricists, such as Hume, to embrace *skepticism*, the view that it is impossible to have knowledge of even the most fundamental kind. Much of philosophy since Hume has been devoted to responding to the problems that generate skepticism.

It is important for our purposes to note how peculiar these problems are. We saw in the last chapter that Dewey criticizes traditional philosophy for its fascination with intellectual puzzles and its depreciation of the world of common experience. Hasn't Dewey's criticism been vindicated in the present discussion? As Dewey has indicated, through its fixation with such problems, philosophy finds itself alienated from the concerns of ordinary life and thus ill equipped to deal with the actual problems that inevitably arise. One is reminded of Hume's confession that he must abandon philosophy when dealing with the world. Hume claims that, despite his skepticism,

> I dine, I play a game of back-gammon, I converse, and am merry with my friends; and when after three or four hours' amusement, I wou'd return to these speculations, they appear so cold, and strain'd, and ridiculous, that I cannot find in my heart to enter into them any farther. Here then I find myself absolutely and necessarily determin'd to live, and talk, and act like other people in the common affairs of life . . . .[10]

Although traditional empiricism begins with the world of "common affairs," it quickly becomes a means of escape from the world, a detached intellectual exercise which concludes that there is no knowledge and that the world with which it began is nonexistent.

Dewey's Theory of Experience

The Idea of a Radically Empirical Theory of Experience

The traditional view creates a dualism between an inner world of sensations and an outer world of objects, and then tries to understand how these two supposedly separate realms are connected. A series of puzzles is thereby generated: Does my experience connect me to the world outside my mind? Is there such a world? Is it possible to have knowledge at all? Philosophy has been occupied with these questions for centuries; in many quarters, these are still considered the philosophical issues *par excellence*. In the last chapter, we discussed Dewey's "test of the value of any philosophy which is offered us." This test, you will remember, consists in determining whether the proposed philosophical theory renders "ordinary life-experiences and their predicaments" more intelligible, "more luminous to us." Let us apply this test to the traditional view of experience. How well does the traditional theory explain experience? Does it render experience "more luminous," or does it make things "more opaque" (*EN*, LW1:18)?

The answer is evident. The traditional view makes experience a mystery. That there is experience is certain, but what experience is, how experience arises, and how it is related to the world at large is not only left unexplained by the traditional theory, but is actually rendered inexplicable by it! Certainly, we should not be satisfied with a theory of experience which terminates in conclusions which make experience *more* obscure, which make the very existence of the world an intractable problem.

What shall we do? We must develop a better view of experience. In developing a new theory, it is important to recognize where the traditional theory went wrong. Dewey's diagnosis is clear, "the traditional accounts [of experience] have not been empirical, but have been deductions, from unnamed premises of what experience *must* be" (MW10:11). Fascinated with the achievement of Issac Newton, who constructed a system of physics out of ultimate, insensible particles of matter in motion, the traditional empiricists sought to develop a theory of experience and knowledge that resembled Newtonian mechanics. In so doing, however, they overlooked the actual features of experience. As such, the traditional view is not empirical enough, it is a theory of experience that is not *derived from* experience. Ask yourself whether the traditional view captures what happens when you look at an apple. Do you *experience* distinct, atomic sensations of deep red? Does your *experience* present itself to you in discrete, disjointed sensory images? Does *experience* lead you to skepticism? Does *experience* lead you to doubt the existence of the world? Notice how many pages of this chapter have been dedicated to articulating the traditional theory. Were it the case that the traditional view actually described what experience is, it should not have been so difficult to explain it. Unless you have some philosophical training, the traditional theory of experience is probably *foreign* to you.

In constructing a new theory of experience, then, we cannot begin with some presupposed notion of what experience "must be"; we instead turn to experience itself. In this sense, Dewey's is a "radically empirical" theory of experience. It is "radically" empirical in that it derives its conception of experience from *experience itself.*[11]

Dewey's Radically Empirical Theory of Experience

Let us begin anew. What is experience? I am again looking at my apple. I reach for it, grasp it, raise it to my mouth, and take another bite. What is striking about these operations is that they occur not as a series of disjointed sensory events (as the traditional view would have it), but rather as a *continuum* of action. I do not first *see* the apple, then *feel* it, and then *taste* it; these visual, tactile, and gustatory aspects are coordinated within the single *activity* of eating the apple. Moreover, the different sensory aspects are adjusted to each other, they constitute a "circuit" of behavior rather than a mere succession of sensations.[12] That is, the seeing of the apple *informs* the reaching and the attempt to grasp it. Subsequently, the grasping is responsive to the effort to bite the apple. Even in the particular aspect of seeing the apple, I am not "presented" with an image; seeing the apple is a *looking*, an inspection. I am not simply being affected by the apple, I am *doing something*; in this case I am *locating* the object that I wish to put in my mouth. Seeing is thus an *action*, not a passive beholding. Further, the seeing that results does not consist in an isolated patch of deep red, I see an apple against a particular background, in a specific position, under certain conditions, and at a certain distance.

What these considerations suggest is that experience is not primarily sensory perception, as the traditional view had proposed. The distinct sensory images that ground the traditional model are actually *abstractions*; they are not "starting points," but postulates, the "products of analysis" (*EN*, LW1:116). Turning away from theory and to an examination of experience itself, we find that the atomic "sensation" of the traditional view is a fiction; sensory images are not "presented" to the mind as the particular frames of a film-strip, they do not exist in isolation. Rather, sensation occurs always within a larger context of a certain *activity*, undertaken within certain conditions and for a certain purpose.

Our examination of experience thus leads us to acknowledge that the "sensation" of the traditional empiricist is *not* primary; rather, what experience suggests about itself is that it is "an affair primarily of doing" (*RP*, MW12:129), it is "an affair of the intercourse of a living being with its physical and social environment" (MW10:6). This "intercourse" must be understood as an *exchange*, a *transaction* in which a live creature and factors within its environment interact. Accordingly, experience involves "an active and a passive element":

> On the active hand, experience is *trying*—a meaning which is made explicit in the connected term experiment. On the passive, it is *undergoing*. When we experience something, we act upon it, we do something with it; then we suffer or undergo the consequences. We do something to the thing and then it does something to us in return. . . . (*DE*, MW9:146)

"Experience, in other words, is a matter of *simultaneous* doings and sufferings" (MW10:9). That experience involves simultaneous action and undergoing indicates that experience is a *continuous* process. More precisely, experience is the continuous process of the interaction of a live creature with other factors within a common environment.

Let's consider another example. Driving a car is an excellent case of experience as Dewey understands the term. When driving, one is not simply "watching," one is not merely being "presented" with the images of the road and the other cars. Driving is an affair of the interaction of the driver with other factors within an environment. Within the environment are the other cars, the surface of the road, the traffic regulations, the weather conditions. Some of these factors are relatively stable, such as the speed limit and the general lay of the road; others are prone to fluctuation, such as the position of the other cars and the weather conditions. When driving, one must *adjust* one's activity to the present conditions. This adjustment is not a passive conformity to the environment—driving requires the *coordination* of action to and with the environment. These actions do not simply modify the driver, they introduce certain changes into the present environment. When one's actions are not well coordinated with the other factors within the environment, a car accident typically results.

Of course, this process of interaction requires sensory perception, but, again, sensory information is not primary and ultimate; the sights and sounds associated with driving are actually *lookings* and *listenings*, they are *actions* performed *for the sake of* driving. As such, the particular sensory aspects of the experience occur within and acquire their significance from the activity of driving the car. They therefore are not simply images "presented" to the mind as a passive receptor, they are associated with a certain *purpose*, they perform a *function*, they serve to coordinate, adjust, inform, and direct action.

Contrasts with the Traditional Theory

With the foregoing sketch of Dewey's theory of experience in mind, we may now identify specific points of contrast between the traditional view and that of Dewey. In his "The Need for a Recovery of Philosophy," Dewey identifies five points of contrast. Following Dewey, we'll take them in turn, briefly commenting on each.[13]

> (*i*) In the orthodox view, experience is regarded primarily as a knowledge-affair. But to the eyes not looking through ancient spectacles, it assuredly appears as an affair of the intercourse of a living being with its physical and social environment. (MW10:6)

The leading disputes of Modern philosophy concern the epistemological value of experience. In this sense, experience has been "regarded primarily as a knowledge-affair," the significance of experience has been taken to consist entirely within its relation to knowledge. On Dewey's view, however, experience is the medium by which the live creature sustains itself; experience is *lived*, it is principally a phenomenon of life, not knowledge. As we'll see in the next chapter, Dewey develops a theory of knowledge according to which knowing is a special *kind* of activity within experience.

> (*ii*) According to tradition experience is (at least primarily) a psychical thing, infected throughout with "subjectivity." What experience suggests about itself is a genuinely objective world which enters into the actions and sufferings of men and undergoes modifications through their responses. (MW10:6)

On the traditional conception, experience is a series of images in the mind. With these mental images taken as the ultimate elements of experience, there naturally arises the problem of the relation between "inner" experience and the "external" world. We thus wondered whether the deep red I perceive when I look at my apple *corresponds* to the apple itself; eventually, we were led to wonder whether there was an apple at all. Dewey argues that such difficulties do not arise out of experience itself, but rather are the *products* of a certain *theory* of experience. Experience does not lead one to deny the existence of an external world; experience suggests that we are creatures that act under certain conditions. These conditions affect our action, and, in acting, we in turn affect the conditions.

> (*iii*) So far as anything beyond a bare present is recognized by the established doctrine, the past exclusively counts. Registration of what has taken place, reference to precedent, is believed to be the essence of experience. Empiricism is conceived of as tied up to what has been, or is "given." But experience in its vital form is experimental, an effort to change the given; it is characterized by projection, by reaching forward into the unknown; connection with the future is its salient trait. (MW10:6)

On the traditional model, experience is the passive receiving of sensory information emitted by objects. As such, experience is construed as a mere record of that which *is*. An experience is epistemologically valuable in the degree to which it is an accurate representation of its object. We have seen how this conception generates epistemological problems. On Dewey's conception, by contrast, experience is not a passively received record of the external world, it is rather an active affair of interaction with the world. Understood as the interactivity of a live creature and other active factors within its environment, experience is primarily concerned with a projected future, a transformed environment. Conditions existing at the moment of perception are not to be simply recorded, they are the materials to be used within the activity of experience.

> (*iv*) The empirical tradition is committed to particularism. Connections and continuities are supposed to be foreign to experience, to be by-products of dubious validity. An experience that is an undergoing of an environment and a striving for its control in new directions is pregnant with connections. (MW10:6)

The experiment conducted earlier demonstrated the outcome of the traditional view's commitment to ultimate and atomic "sensations"; with experience pulverized into discrete, particular elements the *relations* between distinct sensations become inexplicable. This implication led Hume to deny that we could know that there are continuities in experience. Hume argued that the apparent relations between distinct experiences were not features of experience itself, but were actually due to the operations of the mind which habitually generated the illusion of continuity within experience.[14] A radically empirical theory of experience begins with the fact that experience contains continuities and connections. Experience itself occurs as a *continuum* of doings and undergoings; the relations that obtain between different phases within experience are not imported from outside, they are actual features of experience.

> (*v*) In the traditional notion experience and thought are antithetical terms. Inference, so far as it is other than a revival of what has been given in the past, goes beyond experience; hence it is either invalid or else a measure of desperation by which, using experience as a springboard, we jump out to a world of stable things and other selves. But experience, taken free of the restrictions imposed by the older concept, is full of inference. There is, apparently, no conscious experience without inference; reflection is native and constant. (MW10:6)

Because it has defined experience strictly in terms of sensory perception, the traditional theory has generated a dualism between "experience," the procession of mental images, and "thinking" or "reason," a separate faculty of the mind that draws general conclusions ('infers') from particular experiences. With experience understood as just so many distinct and unrelated sensory events, the operation by which they were organized and used in deriving conclusions were rendered suspect. Dewey's theory, however, is committed to no such dualism between the original stuff of experience and the faculty that organizes it. "Thinking," understood by Dewey not simply as the abstract logical operation of "inference" but as the activity of *directing* behavior with reference to present conditions, does not exist apart from experience, it is an operation *within* it.

By means of this contrast, we have arrived at a reasonably complete understanding of Dewey's theory of experience. This conception provides the basis for the rest of Dewey's philosophy.[15] Having seen that the traditional theory cannot provide a fruitful epistemology, we next turn to the new variety of empiricism that Dewey constructs with his theory of experience.

Summary

The competing schools in the history of philosophy share a common theory of experience. As this theory generates all of the standard philosophical dualisms and their corresponding problems, the effort to reconstruct philosophy must begin with the reconstruction of the theory of experience.

We began by sketching in some detail the main features of the traditional conception of experience. On this theory, experience is understood to consist in distinct, atomic mental images ("sensations") generated via sensory perception. We encountered a number of problems which arise from this view, and saw that such problems lead one ultimately to skepticism. Following Dewey, we decided that we ought not to be satisfied with a theory of experience that rendered experience itself inexplicable.

In framing a new theory of experience, we adopted Dewey's stance of "radical empiricism." That is, we turned to *experience itself* to derive our theory of experience. Through an examination of experience, we discovered that experience is not a procession of discrete sensory images, but rather consists in a *continuum* of behavior. Consequently, experience is not to be understood as the reception of mental representations of an external world, experience is primarily the activity of interaction involving a live creature and other factors within an environment. Whereas the traditional theory took experience to be a passive affair of the mind being presented with particular images of the "external" world, the radically empirical theory associates experience with the life activities of an organism. The chapter concluded with a discussion of five points of contrast between the traditional view and Dewey's theory.

We began the chapter noting that Dewey is a kind of empiricist. With Dewey's reconstructed theory of experience in place, we are now ready to examine Dewey's reconstruction of the theory of knowledge.

Endnotes

[1] Epistemology is the area of philosophy concerned with issues regarding the nature and possibility of knowledge. What is knowledge? How is it gained? Is it possible to know anything? These are the standard questions that epistemologists ask.

[2] The Modern period in the history of philosophy runs roughly from the late sixteenth century to the twentieth century.

[3] See the first of his *Meditations on First Philosophy* (Cambridge: Cambridge University Press, 1996). Descartes' argument is that every sensory experience you are having right now—that you are reading this sentence, for example—is consistent with the claim that you are *dreaming* that you are having that experience. You may right now be dreaming that your are reading this sentence. If you are now dreaming, you cannot be reading, because your eyes are closed!

[4] John Locke, *An Essay Concerning Human Understanding* (Nidditch edition, Oxford: Clarendon Press, 1975), 104.

[5] See Locke's *Essay* (*ibid.*), 136. See also Bertrand Russell's *The Problems of Philosophy* (London: Oxford University Press, 1959), and Charles Landesman's *Introduction to Epistemology* (Cambridge: Blackwell, 1997), Chs. 1-3.

[6] See the First Part of Kant's *Prolegomena to Any Future Metaphysics* (New York: Macmillan, 1950) for a discussion of the "thing in itself."

[7] The following example was suggested to me by Robert Buckley.
[8] See the first of his *Three Dialogues* (In Berkeley's *Philosophical Works*, Michael Ayers, ed. London: J. M. Dent Publishers, 1993).
[9] See Book One of Hume's *Treatise of Human Nature* (Selby-Bigge edition, Oxford: Clarendon Press, 1978). See also Hume's *Enquiry Concerning Human Understanding* (Selby-Bigge edition, Oxford: Clarendon Press, 1975), especially sections 2-5.
[10] Hume, *A Treatise of Human Nature (ibid.)*, 269.
[11] The term 'radical' is cognate to the Latin word for "root." It is in this sense that I'm claiming that Dewey's theory of experience is "radically empirical"—it attempts to use experience to go to the root of experience. The term 'radical empiricism' was coined by William James; one may consult his *Essays in Radical Empiricism* (Cambridge: Harvard University Press, 1975), especially his "A World of Pure Experience," for his expression of the view. I here employ the term in a way which differs somewhat from James's use.
[12] The discussion that follows draws heavily from Dewey's 1896 paper, "The Reflex Arc Concept in Psychology" (EW5:96-109). In this essay Dewey rejects the "disjointed psychology" (EW5:99) of traditional empiricism and develops the concept of a "circuit" of coordinated activity.
[13] I refer the reader to Richard Bernstein's excellent discussions of the following passages in chapter 5 of his *John Dewey* (California: Ridgeview Publishing, 1966), 57-74.
[14] See especially Sections 4 and 5 of Hume's *Enquiry* (*ibid.*).
[15] It is important to note in this connection that three of Dewey's most important works feature the word 'experience' in the title: *Experience and Nature*, *Art as Experience*, and *Experience and Education*.

4
Reconstructing Knowledge

Dewey and the Epistemological Tradition

The Problems of Epistemology

In the preceding chapter, we encountered three problems that are paradigmatically epistemological. First, we confronted what is broadly known as the "problem of knowledge." This problem arises out of the realization that since experience, as it is traditionally understood, consists in distinct mental images, there is no way to verify within experience the relation of one's experience to the world outside. As knowledge is taken to consist in having one's experience *accurately* represent the world, it is impossible to know that one has knowledge. Once the connection between our experiences and the world is severed, a second problem known as the "problem of the external world" arises. If experience is always experience *of* mental images, and if all knowledge is derived from experience, it is impossible to know that there is a world external to and independent of one's experience.

These two problems lead directly to the most persistent problem in epistemology, namely, the "problem of skepticism." Noting that even the most fundamental beliefs cannot be established as knowledge, the skeptic denies the possibility of knowledge altogether. The skeptic promotes his position by challenging those who claim to have knowledge to *prove* that they know. Of course, any attempt to meet the skeptic's challenge will have to *presume* some knowledge; for it is clear that a proof consists in establishing, on the basis of some *premises* which are *assumed* true, the truth of some conclusion. Once a proof is given, the skeptic will ask for proofs for each of the premises employed in the original proof.[1] Any attempt to meet the skeptical challenge will therefore result only in more grist for the skeptic's mill. Consequently, the skeptic can show that most common sense beliefs are entirely unfounded.[2]

Philosophers since Descartes have been captivated by such problems, and many of the major works of Modern philosophy are explicitly addressed to epistemological topics. In fact, all the main epistemological schools of the Modern period can be understood as different attempts to resolve the problems described above.

Dewey, by contrast, does not endeavor to respond to the questions and problems of traditional epistemology. Dewey instead asks,

> Is it not time that philosophers turned from the attempt to determine the comparative merits of various replies to the questions [of epistemology] to a consideration of the claims of the questions? (MW10:24)

Dewey is confident that once philosophers make such a turn, they will discover that "the trouble is with the problem[s]" (MW10:25); they will find that the problems of epistemology are "blocks to inquiry, blind alleys" (*EN*, LW1:17), they will agree that we do not "solve" such problems, we "get over" them (MW4:14).[3] Dewey's insistence that philosophers should abandon the problems of traditional epistemology rests upon his argument that these problems arise only if one accepts a series of obsolete assumptions about the nature of knowledge. That is, Dewey maintains that the clash between the traditional schools of epistemology has been concerned strictly with differing views about how knowledge is *acquired*; all the traditional theories nevertheless agree upon a certain conception of what knowledge *is*. Dewey's strategy is to expose and criticize this common view of knowledge. With this view disposed of, a reconstructed theory which Dewey called "experimentalism" can be developed.[4]

Dispelling the Spectator

> All the rivalries and connected problems [of epistemology] grow from a single root. They spring from the assumption that the true and valid object of knowledge is that which has being prior to and independent of the operations of knowing. They spring from the doctrine that knowledge is a grasp or beholding of reality without anything being done to modify its antecedent state . . . . (*QC*, LW4:157)

In the above quotation, Dewey identifies the conception of knowledge that underlies traditional epistemology. Dewey famously baptized this conception the "spectator theory of knowledge." This view of knowledge evokes the image of a spectator on two levels. First, the traditional view adopts a metaphysical dualism between the knowing "subject" and the "object" that is known; standing apart from the objects known, the knower is a "spectator," an "outsider."[5] Second, knowing is conceived as a passive affair of the "object" of knowledge being "presented to" the knower; the knowing subject is "wholly passive and acquiescent in knowing" (*RP*, MW12:128), and is thus a "spectator" in the sense of "non-participant."

According to Dewey, the spectator view results from the assumptions of a psychological theory that has been "exploded" by current advances in biology. According to this obsolete psychology,

> Mental life originated in sensations which are separately and passively received, and which are formed, through laws of retention and association, into a mosaic of images perceptions, conceptions. (*RP*, MW12:128)

Accordingly, philosophers inherited the idea that "knowledge is intrinsically a mere beholding or viewing of reality" (*RP*, MW12:144). Hence traditional epistemologies share a common feature:

> The theory of knowing is modeled after what was supposed to take place in the act of vision. The object refracts light to the eye and is seen: it makes a difference to the eye and to the person having an optical apparatus, but none to the thing seen. The real object is the object so fixed in its regal aloofness that it is a king to any beholding mind that may gaze upon it. (*QC*, LW4:19)

Given such assumptions, "A spectator theory of knowledge is the inevitable outcome" (*QC*, LW4:19). With the senses regarded "as gateways or avenues of knowledge" (*RP*, MW12:128) and knowledge construed as a spectator's detached beholding of an "external" and fixed Reality, all the puzzles of traditional epistemology arise.

On the spectator view, the knower is an ideal *observer*, a passive *surveyor* of a Reality which exists apart from the knower and the act of knowing. It is this picture of the knower that is rendered untenable by contemporary science, and is therefore in need of reconstruction. As was discussed earlier, Dewey takes Darwinian biology to be the scientific paradigm *par excellence*; the notion of a live creature thus always underlies his reconstructive efforts. Dewey writes:

> The effect of the development of biology has been to reverse the [traditional] picture. Wherever there is life, there is behavior, activity. In order that life may persist, this activity has to be both continuous and adapted to the environment. This adaptive adjustment, moreover, is not wholly passive; it is not a mere matter of the molding of the organism by the environment . . . . There is no such thing in a living creature as mere conformity to conditions . . . . In the interests of the maintenance of life there is transformation of some elements in the surrounding medium. (*RP*, MW12:128)

From these Darwinian considerations, "Certain important implications for philosophy follow":

> The interaction of organism and environment, resulting in some adaptation which secures utilization of the latter, is the primary fact. . . Knowledge is relegated to a derived position, secondary in origin, even if its importance, when once established, is overshadowing. Knowledge is not something separate and self-sufficing, but it is involved in the process by which life is sustained and evolved. (RP, MW12:129)

Like the traditional empiricists' atomic sensations encountered in the last chapter, the spectator of traditional epistemology is a fiction. Unless we are to cling to an archaic psychological theory, we must reject traditional epistemology's metaphysical dualism between a detached "inner" knower and the "external" world that is known. Instead, we must acknowledge that the knower and the known occupy a common world—the knower is not a ghostly "outsider" looking in on Reality, but a creature living within an environment. Hence, the knower is not a passive recipient of sensations; rather, the knower is *essentially* an organism, an *agent* which lives by means of transaction within its environment. Therefore, we must reject any epistemology which makes knowledge into something "separate and self-sufficing" by divorcing it from the life-sustaining behavior of the live creature.

Moreover, the rejection of the spectator image entails the rejection of the traditional conception of the object of knowledge. According to the spectator theory, what is known is a fixed and static Reality in "regal aloofness."[6] If we accept Dewey's Darwinian picture, however, we are "forced to abandon the assumption of fixity" *(RP*, MW12:260); we must acknowledge that there is no "Reality" apart from environments, and that environments are mutable, dynamic, and in *process*. Accordingly, we must abandon any epistemological theory which postulates an immutable Reality as the proper object of knowledge. Instead, knowledge must be understood in terms of the live creature's interaction with its dynamic environment.

The conclusion to be drawn is that traditional epistemology ought to be abandoned on the grounds that its entire enterprise rests upon untenable presuppositions. Whereas some have taken this negative stance to be the whole of Dewey's message,[7] we must now turn to an examination of Dewey's proposal for a new epistemology.

The Experimental Theory of Knowing

The Source of a New Epistemology

We must *reconstruct* the theory of knowledge. How shall we begin? Before attempting to propose a new theory, it is important to consider the failings of traditional epistemology. To this end, let's risk redundancy and briefly review a few points made in Chapter Three, where we examined Dewey's critique of traditional philosophy.

Central to this critique is Dewey's argument that philosophy originated from the cultural need to integrate traditional values and science. Traditional philosophies attempted to achieve this integration through the introduction of dualisms of various kinds. Particularly, traditional philosophies feature a *metaphysical* dualism between a changeless, eternal Reality and the changing, imperfect world of ordinary affairs. This initial dualism generates an *epistemological* dualism between the kind of knowledge associated with these different metaphysical realms. The realm of perfect Being is accessed only through the rational contemplation associated with philosophical speculation. Experience and observation, by contrast, provides knowledge of the inferior realm of physical objects and ordinary affairs. With true Reality elevated to a metaphysical realm which could not be accessed by scientific observation, but is revealed only to the philosopher, the objects in the world of experience and the methods employed by the scientist were rendered subordinate. Consequently, the traditional values and attitudes were preserved.[8]

Dewey's criticism is that now, in light of the overwhelming success of the scientific method, philosophy must take the opposite path. As always, philosophy is to perform the social function of integrating cultural values with developing science and technology, but a reconstructed philosophy must pursue this integration through the *extension* of the methods and attitudes of science to culture itself. Philosophy must become the mode of social criticism by which traditional culture becomes more scientific. Consequently, philosophy itself must become more scientific by purging itself of the scientifically obsolete presuppositions it has inherited from its past.

Traditional epistemology has understood knowledge to be a matter of passively receiving accurate representations of a static and complete Reality. Since the sixteenth century, however, science has been developing an alternate model according to which knowledge is essentially the "active and operative" affair of "experiment guided by hypothesis" (*RP*, MW12:150).[9] That is, science is not essentially concerned with *representing* the world, with getting an accurate *image* of Reality; rather science understands knowledge to be the practical affair of *predicting* and *controlling* the changing course of nature.

Since a reconstructed philosophy must align itself with science, philosophers can no longer take epistemology to be independent of science. A reconstructed epistemology must model its conception of knowledge on the methods of experimentation employed in the sciences.[10] Hence Dewey referred to his view as "experimentalism."

Epistemology Reconstructed: Knowing as Inquiry

Thus far, we have been discussing Dewey's *approach* to the theory of knowledge; we have examined his critique of traditional epistemology and outlined his idea of what a reconstructed epistemology must do. Now we must develop Dewey's proposal. Since a reconstructed epistemology is to be modeled after scientific inquiry, Dewey described his epistemology as a "theory of inquiry."[11]

What is inquiry? We again begin with experience. You will recall that Dewey understands experience to be the activity of an organism interacting with certain factors within an environment that is both precarious and stable. In his principal work on inquiry, *Logic: The Theory of Inquiry* (LW12), Dewey introduces the term 'situation' to denote the physical and social aspects of the environment, the "contextual whole" (*LI*, LW12:72) within which experience occurs. As situations are dynamic and prone to fluctuation, the live creature is occasionally confronted with instability, danger, and obstruction. In such cases, the organism is operating within what Dewey calls an "indeterminate situation" (*LI*, LW12:109). On Dewey's view, inquiry is a certain kind of activity within experience which occurs when the organism encounters an indeterminate situation. Precisely, inquiry is,

> . . . the controlled or directed transformation of an indeterminate situation into one that is so determinate in its constituent distinctions and relations as to convert the elements of the original situation into a unified whole. (*LI*, LW12:108)

That is, the indeterminate situation presents the organism with a *problem*. The activity of addressing the problem by means of action directed towards the *transformation* of the existing situation is *inquiry*. Inquiry is successful if it transforms the problematic situation into a "unified whole," a "determinate situation" (*LI*, LW12:109).

With inquiry generally understood as the live creature's response to a problematic situation, we recognize that, because there are many kinds of problem, inquiry occurs at several levels. One can think of large-scale inquiry into a global problem such as the depletion of the ozone layer, or more local inquiries into paltry problems such as when I forget where I left my car keys. Despite the varying subject-matter and gravity of different inquiries, Dewey maintains that there is a general pattern which all successful inquiry follows (*LI*, LW12:105). The general pattern of inquiry can be expressed in five steps, they are:

> (1) Perplexity, confusion, doubt, due to the fact that one is implicated in an incomplete situation whose full character is not yet determined;
>
> (2) A conjectural anticipation—a tentative interpretation of the given elements, attributing to them a tendency to effect certain consequences;
>
> (3) A careful survey (examination, inspection, exploration, analysis) of all attainable consideration which will define and clarify the problem in hand;
>
> (4) A consequent elaboration of the tentative hypothesis to make it more precise and more consistent, because squaring it with a wider range of facts;
>
> (5) Taking one stand upon the projected hypothesis as a plan of action which is applied to the existing state of affairs: doing something overtly to bring about the anticipated result, and thereby testing the hypothesis. (*DE*, MW9:157)[12]

Dewey is not suggesting that in every inquiry, one performs five distinct operations, nor is Dewey proposing that the phases occur in a serial order. Different steps may "telescope together" and inform each other (*HT*, LW6:238). In some cases, the distinct phases are easily discriminated whereas in others they occur all at once.

An example would be instructive. In the last chapter, we considered driving as a paradigmatic case of Deweyan experience, for it is clearly a matter of dynamic interaction and continual coordination within a particular situation. Let's now suppose you're driving down a residential street in a small town. Parked cars line the street on both sides, obscuring your vision of the houses. It's a sunny, warm day, and you're especially enjoying the music playing on the radio. These factors—the parked cars, the road, the houses, the weather conditions, the time of day, your enjoyment of the music—are all part of the situation within which you are driving. Of course, we could identify further constituent features: the traffic laws, the speed at which you are driving, your mood, the weight of your car, your reflexive abilities, etc. Remember, by "situation" Dewey means the "contextual whole" of an "environing experienced world" (*LI*, LW12:72), so our description of any situation can become rather complex!

The situation, as we have described it, is non-problematic—you are simply *driving* the car without really thinking about it, you're on "automatic pilot" as we sometimes say. Now suppose that in the distance, you see a ball suddenly roll into the street. Within this particular situation, the ball marks the institution of indeterminacy; the situation has become "uncertain, unsettled, [and] disturbed" (*LI*, LW12:109), and inquiry begins. It is important to note that "it is the *situation* that has these traits"; "*We* are doubtful because the situation is inherently doubtful" (*LI*, LW12:109). The perplexity and confusion is not an "inner" state of one's mind; on Dewey's view, inquiry begins when the *world*, the situation, becomes disordered and indeterminate. Note also that the indeterminacy does not consist solely in the appearance of the physical ball; it rather has to do with certain *social* features of the situation. A ball in the street *means* that children are playing, and children are not always cautious. As we live within a society which values the lives of children, one is likely to want to avoid hitting a child with one's car. Certainly, we could imagine a society in which children did not play with balls, or which did not value the lives of its children; in such cases, the ball in the street would have a different *meaning*, and might not be problematic at all.

You develop the following interpretation of the problem: "Children are playing with a ball which has gotten away from them; a child is likely to dart out into the street after it without checking the traffic. If I do not do something, I run the risk of hitting a child with my car, which is something I want to avoid." You survey the conditions. Noting that the ball is still a good distance from your car, you propose that the problem can be solved if you slow your car down and wait for the child. You thus begin to *act* in certain ways to introduce certain changes into the situation. For instance, you will probably apply the brakes, focus your vision in the direction from which the ball came, perhaps you will lower the volume of the radio and listen for the sounds of children at play. Note that these actions constitute a *transformation* of the existing situation. As your car crawls along, the child runs into the street for the ball, retrieves it, and returns to play. Your hypothesis has been confirmed, the indeterminate situation has been transformed. Inquiry ceases. You continue driving.

Of course, in cases like the one just considered, the different phases of inquiry are discriminable as distinct steps only after the fact. If you've ever had an experience like the one described, you know that things tend to happen so quickly that one is not *aware* of the individual operations conducted. Consideration of another example will help highlight the distinct steps in inquiry.

Cases of what we call "troubleshooting" are good examples of inquiry. A few days ago, I tried to call a friend. I picked up my telephone, but, to my surprise, there was no dial tone on the line. I was thus confronted with a problem, a disordered situation; moreover, it was a particular *kind* of problem—the situation was not a total chaos—the situation was problematic insofar as I could not make my call. I surveyed the conditions to clarify the problem: Had I paid my phone bill? Yes. Was the phone broken? It did not appear so. I arrived at the hypothesis that there was no dial tone because I had left the other extension of the line off the hook. Were this the case, then I should be able to go to the other extension, return the receiver to the hook, pick it up again, and make my call. I therefore conducted this rudimentary experiment—I walked to the other room and discovered that the extension was not off the hook. My hypothesis had failed.

I was now confronted with a *new* problem, there was no dial tone, but the extension was not off the hook. I had misdiagnosed the situation. I had to reinterpret the situation, and inquiry began again.

In this case, the distinct phases of inquiry are easy to identify. (1) When I picked up my phone, I was confronted with surprise and mild perplexity. (2) Almost instantly, I developed an interpretation of the situation that located the problematic elements: there was no dial tone. (3) I quickly surveyed possible causes of this problem; I decided that the most plausible hypothesis is that I had left the other extension off the hook. (4) I then elaborated the hypothesis, realizing that if the extension were off the hook, I should then be able to walk to the other room, find the extension off the hook, return it to the hook, and get a dial tone. (5) I then acted on this hypothesis, and in so doing, I tested it. I walked to the other room and found the extension on the hook. The experiment had disconfirmed my hypothesis; I returned to step (2)—I reinterpreted the situation—and inquiry continued.

The foregoing discussions of inquiry might sound almost too commonsensical to warrant philosophical attention. Recalling Dewey's "test for the value of any philosophy that is offered us" (*EN*, LW1:18), we realize that Dewey *wants* to propose a theory of knowledge that captures the ordinary, common sense cases of problem-solving within experience. However, our familiarity with the pattern of inquiry should not suggest that Dewey's proposal is lacking in philosophical import. Dewey's theory is rich with implications. To these we now turn.

Aspects of the Experimental Theory

The most significant features of Dewey's theory are captured in the term we used to designate it, "the experimental theory of knowing." On Dewey's view, the concern of epistemology is not "knowledge," but *knowing*, the *activity* of *transforming* problematic situations, the process of "inquiry." Inquiry is conducted in response to a problematic situation, the *objective* of inquiry is the solved problem, the transformed situation. Accordingly, inquiry is a matter of developing *hypotheses* and performing *experimental* operations within an indeterminate situation. There is no guarantee prior to hypothesis-directed action that the proposed solution will be successful in restoring order to the situation. As in the case of my phone, hypotheses can fail to resolve the problem. Thus, knowing as inquiry is essentially *experimental*; in inquiry, hypotheses are tested by experimental action. Whereas defeated hypotheses are revised or abandoned, successful hypotheses are *confirmed*, but not accepted as fixed and final formulations of the "truth." A successful hypothesis is considered "warranted" for use in directing further inquiry, and therefore is always revisable, fallible, subject to the test of future inquiry.[13]

In this sense, the experimental theory of knowing is consistent with the practices of science. As you may have realized, the pattern of inquiry resembles a standard treatment of the scientific method. It is important to note that, according to Dewey, science is *continuous* with everyday inquiry. As we saw in Chapter Three, Dewey maintains that "science" in the sense of persons wearing white coats performing sophisticated experiments in laboratories is an *extension* of more basic activity originating in the activities of artisans and craftsmen.

The transition from a spectator theory of knowledge to an experimental theory of knowing thus involves a series of significant conceptual shifts. According to the experimentalist, knowing is not a state of intellectually perceiving Reality. The experimentalist does not think of knowledge "after the model of a spectator viewing a finished picture," but rather takes knowing to consist in the abilities of controlled action associated with "the artist producing the painting" (*RP*, MW12:150). Knowing is thus a *skill*, an *ability* to direct and control situations. To have "knowledge" is to be capable of *doing something*. Specifically, it is the ability to act in ways which introduce "certain determinate changes in the world" (*DE*, MW9:158) which direct the course of developing situations toward an envisioned result.

Moreover, unlike the traditional epistemologist, who understood the object of knowledge to be a fixed and static "external world," the experimentalist recognizes that "the knower is within the world of existence"; inquiry therefore "marks an interaction of one existence with other existences," a "transitional redirection and rearrangement of the real" (*QC*, LW4:235-236). That is, the "object of knowledge" is not a standing external reality, but the *transformed* situation.[14] The outcome of successful inquiry is therefore not "knowledge" in the traditional sense, but confirmed hypotheses, "warranted assertions," an increased ability to conduct successful inquiry in the future. This ability is what Dewey calls "intelligence."

The Purpose of the Experimental Theory

A central aspect of experimentalism is that it abandons the traditional view that knowledge is somehow a self-sufficing end in itself. On the experimental view, knowing is always a *practical* affair of addressing problems within experience; the value of knowing is therefore *instrumental*. As such, the theory of inquiry has a *purpose*, a job to perform within the context of Dewey's general reconstructive program of directing the focus of philosophy away from the traditional puzzles and towards the "problems of men."

The theory of inquiry is the key to philosophical reconstruction. With knowing understood to be a matter of employing the right kind of method in dealing with problems, the general pattern of inquiry can be applied to *moral* and *social* problems. According to Dewey,

> . . . reconstruction can be nothing less than the work of developing, of forming, of producing (in the literal sense of that word) the intellectual instrumentalities which will

> progressively direct inquiry into the deeply and inclusively human—that is to say, moral—facts of the present scene and situation. (*RP*, MW12:269)

One of the features of the spectator theory of knowledge was the view that questions of human values were beyond the reach of scientific inquiry. Once the spectator theory is rejected, and an experimental theory adopted, we see that there is no reason to accept this limitation on the powers of inquiry. The final step in reconstruction is the application of experimental inquiry to problems regarding value. In a famous passage, Dewey writes:

> The time will come when it will be found passing strange that we of this age should take such pains to control by every means at command the formation of ideas of physical things, even those most remote from human concern, and yet are content with haphazard beliefs about the qualities of objects that regulate our deepest interests; that we are scrupulous as to methods of forming ideas of natural objects, and either dogmatic or else driven by immediate conditions in framing those about values. (*QC*, LW4:214)

In the next chapter we shall examine Dewey's attempt to bring experimental inquiry to bear on questions of morality.

Summary

The puzzles of epistemology have been among the most attractive intellectual diversions in the history of philosophy. Dewey identifies and attacks the conception of knowledge common to the traditional epistemological schools. This conception, which Dewey calls the "spectator theory of knowledge," understands knowledge to consist in a detached mind's accurate beholding of a static and external Reality. Dewey rejects the spectator view on the grounds that it rests upon an archaic and obsolete psychological theory according to which the mind is a passive receiver of information about the world. Dewey argues that recent advances in biology render the spectator view untenable; the knower is not essentially a detached mind, but rather an organism which lives within and by means of an environment. A reconstructed theory of knowledge is thus called for.

Dewey's reconstructed epistemology is best described as an "experimental theory of knowing." On Dewey's view, knowing does not consist in the passive apprehension of a detached spectator, but the activity of a live creature in response to a problematic situation. This process of actively responding to a problem is what Dewey calls "inquiry." According to an experimental theory, knowing consists in the *ability* of the organism to conduct successful inquiry. We next turn to Dewey's application of the experimental theory to moral problems.

Endnotes

[1] This argument was first proposed by the ancient skeptic, Sextus Empiricus; it is often referred to as the "problem of the criterion." See *Outlines of Pyrrhonism* (Cambridge: Harvard University Press, 1976).
[2] Those interested in skepticism may consult Richard Popkin's *The History of Skepticism* (Berkeley: University of California Press, 1979).
[3] A similar approach can be found in Ludwig Wittgenstein's *On Certainty* (New York: Harper, 1972).
[4] Consult Dewey's 1909 essay, "The Experimental Theory of Knowledge" (MW3) and Dewey's "Introduction" to his *Essays in Experimental Logic* (MW10; also in Hester and Talisse, eds. *Dewey's Essays in Experimental Logic*. (*ibid.*)).
[5] Keeping with his metaphilosophical principle that philosophical ideas have their source in cultural conditions, Dewey suggests that the spectator theory has its origin in the theological view that the human soul is a "stranger and a pilgrim in this world" (MW10:25).
[6] Recall Plato's argument, discussed in Chapter Three, that Reality, and hence the objects of knowledge, must be unchanging and eternal.
[7] Richard Rorty has repeatedly enlisted Dewey's support for his own campaign against epistemology. See, for example, Rorty's "Science as Solidarity" (in Rorty, *Objectivity, Relativism, and Truth*. Cambridge: Cambridge University Press, 1991). Many have argued that Rorty's reading of Dewey ignores Dewey's attempts to rehabilitate philosophy. James Gouinlock's "What is the Legacy of Instrumentalism?" (in Saatkamp, ed. *Rorty and Pragmatism* (*ibid.*)) features an especially lucid canvass of the current debate.

[8] Plato often characterizes his World of Ideas as the "invisible" realm. In the famous 'divided line' of the *Republic*, the "intelligible" realm is set over and against the "visible" realm (509e).
[9] In *Reconstruction*, Dewey credits Francis Bacon (1561-1626) with being the "real founder of modern thought" (*RP*, MW12:95), and the "prophet of a pragmatic conception of knowledge" (*RP*, MW12:100). Bacon is most famous for the claim that "knowledge is power."
[10] This approach is taken by the influential contemporary philosopher, W. V. Quine. See Quine's "Epistemology Naturalized" (*Ontological Relativity and Other Essays.* New York: Columbia University Press, 1969). The main positions in the current debate regarding Quine's Deweyan approach are expressed in Hilary Kornblith, ed. *Naturalizing Epistemology* (Massachusetts: MIT Press, 1985).
[11] Dewey fully develops his theory in his 1938 *Logic: The Theory of Inquiry* (LW12). The *Logic* is a notoriously daunting book, and we can here engage in only the most basic exposition of Dewey's view. For a collection of current essays on Dewey's logic, see Tom Burke, D. Micah Hester, and Robert Talisse, eds. *New Essays on Dewey's Logical Theory* (Tennessee: Vanderbilt University Press, forthcoming).
[12] Cf. *HT*, MW6:236-237; *HT*, LW8:200-209; and *LI*, LW12:109-122.
[13] In his *Logic*, Dewey coins the term "warranted assertability" as a substitute for the traditional epistemologists' "knowledge" and "truth"; see (*LI*, LW12:15-17).
[14] Dewey's view that the act of knowledge *constructs* its own objects has seemed paradoxical to many commentators. We cannot here examine this claim. Georges Dicker's *Dewey's Theory of Knowing* (Philadelphia: Philosophical Monographs, 1976), and H. S. Thayer's "Objects of Knowledge" (in John Stuhr, ed. *Philosophy and the Reconstruction of Culture.* Albany: SUNY Press, 1993) provide the best analyses of this aspect of Dewey's epistemology.

5
Reconstructing Society

> The problem of restoring integration and cooperation between man's beliefs about the world in which he lives and his beliefs about the values and purposes that should direct his conduct is the deepest problem of modern life. It is the problem of any philosophy that is not isolated from that life. (*QC*, LW4:204)

Dewey's accounts of experience and knowing form the fulcrum of his philosophy. In developing these ideas, we have toured some of the most arduous territory; it might have seemed that, despite Dewey's insistence that philosophy must address the "problems of men," our discussion would never touch ground and enter the world of human affairs. With the essentials now in place, however, we are at last ready to examine the moral and political implications of Dewey's reconstructed philosophy. Philosophers often draw a hard distinction between moral philosophy, more formally known as 'ethics', and political philosophy. Ethics, it is said, is concerned with how the individual acts whereas political philosophy addresses questions regarding the power of the state. On Dewey's view, however, the moral and political are dual aspects of a single concern: community. It would therefore be inappropriate to discuss these topics separately.

Reconstructing Moral Theory

The Inner and the Outer

Throughout this study, we have repeatedly encountered a basic dualism between a non-material, unchanging realm of perfect Being known through Reason and an imperfect, material, and perishing world accessed through experience. As one might expect, this fundamental disjunction finds an analogue in moral theory. Modern philosophy has produced two rival theories of morality corresponding to the metaphysical and epistemological dualisms previously met. Accordingly, we may discuss traditional moral theory in terms of a basic dualism between the "inner" and the "outer" (*DE*, MW9:356ff.).

Immanuel Kant (1724-1804) is the principal proponent of what we shall call the "inner" strand in traditional moral theory. According to Kant, the human *will*—viz., the principle of volition, the source and generator of action—is the ultimate object of moral evaluation. Kant famously begins his *Foundations of the Metaphysics of Morals*[1] with the claim, "Nothing in the world—indeed nothing even beyond the world—can possibly be conceived which could be called good without qualification except a *GOOD WILL*" (9). He further argues that the goodness of the will consists not in its ability to direct action towards the correct ends; rather, the good will is good "in itself." Kant writes,

> The good will is not good because of what it effects or accomplishes or because of its competence to achieve some intended end; it is good only because of its willing . . . . (10)

That is, the goodness of the good will is derived not from the consequences of the actions it produces, but simply in virtue of the *character* of its willing. Put more simply, the will is good if its willing is determined by the correct kind of *motive*. According to Kant, the will is correctly motivated if it is obedient to a transcendental Moral Law apprehended by a non-empirical faculty of pure Reason.

Hence the "inner" character of Kant's theory—the will and its motives, as Kant understands them, are mental phenomena.[2] They are not observable and are to be evaluated independently of the observable actions they produce. In Kant's words, moral evaluation is concerned not with the "actions which one sees" but with "their inner principles which one does not see" (23).

We should be suspicious of a moral theory that places the object of moral evaluation out of the reach of observation, especially since it implies that one cannot know the character of one's *own* will, one's own "inner principles." If the will is good insofar as it is properly motivated, and if motives are unobservable, it is impossible for one to know whether one has a good will. It therefore is unclear whether anyone ever acts morally.[3] It might seem, then, that such a theory could not offer sufficient guidance in action.[4]

The utilitarianism of John Stuart Mill (1806-1873) is a paradigmatic example of a moral theory which emphasizes the "outer" tendency.[5] Unlike Kant's theory, utilitarianism places the object of moral evaluation in the "outer" world of experience; actions are evaluated according to their ability to produce certain *consequences*. According to Mill, "actions are right in proportion as they tend to promote happiness; wrong as they tend to produce the reverse of happiness" (7). On the utilitarian view, one ought to perform those actions which *maximize* happiness. Of course, this principle is not very informative until we are told what "happiness" is; according to the utilitarian, happiness consists in "pleasure and the absence of pain" (7). As pain is bad no matter who is suffering it, and pleasure is good no matter who is enjoying it, utilitarianism requires one to maximize *overall* pleasure and minimize *overall* pain in the world. Hence, the utilitarian is committed to the "greatest happiness principle": one ought to perform those actions which result in the greatest happiness *for the greatest number of persons possible.*

Thus, utilitarianism locates moral value not in a transcendental, realm of Reason and "inner principles," but in the degree to which desires are satisfied in the world. To the extent that utilitarianism is empirical, it is an improvement over the Kantian theory. Yet this theory, too, harbors difficulties. According to utilitarianism, each of us ultimately desires "happiness," pleasure without pain. The utilitarian thus takes the satisfaction of desire—the production of pleasure—to be the proper moral aim of action. This view, however, places our specific desires, those activities which we find pleasurable, out of the bounds of moral evaluation. Since actions are morally evaluated according to how well they produce satisfaction, there is no mechanism within the theory for *evaluating* specific desires. It may occur to us that there are some states of affairs that are inherently *not* desirable, despite the fact that some or perhaps most persons might take pleasure in them; some people desire bad things, they derive pleasure from the wrong sources. Some desires are not desir*able*, some people desire things they ought not desire. Utilitarians cannot recognize the distinction between what a person in fact desires and what it is *good* for a person to desire.[6]

Therefore, neither style of moral theory is acceptable. Reconstruction begins once it is realized that both the "inner" and the "outer" varieties of moral theory rest upon common premises which should be abandoned (*RP*, MW12:172). In the first place, we note that underlying the traditional theories is an assumed dualism between the "inner," psychological world of motives and the "outer," physical world of actions. This dualism led the "inner" theories to locate the object of moral evaluation within the unobservable, non-empirical world of a transcendental faculty of Reason; it led the "outer" theories to associate moral value with the satisfaction of existing desires, whatever they may be. Consequently, moral philosophy oscillates,

> . . . between a theory that, in order to save the objectivity of judgments of values, isolates them from experience and nature, and a theory that, in order to save their concrete and human significance, reduces them to mere statements about our own feelings. (*QC*, LW4:210)

The dualism that generates this state of affairs is the product of a psychological theory that is no longer acceptable; a reconstructed moral theory must begin with the live creature. Accordingly, we cannot maintain a dualism between the "inner" factors in behavior and their "outer" expressions; rather, we begin with the *continuity* of motive and act, the *integration* of the organism and its environment. The so-called "inner principles" which determine action are not independent of or prior to action; they are habits and dispositions which have arisen in the course of prior experience, previous action. As such, the supposed dualism of the "inner" and the "outer" is misguided; there is a continuity between habit and act within the experience of the live creature. Again, the behavior of the live creature exhibits the character of a *circuit*; habits are customary modes of response that have been generated in previous action, present actions are guided by habits. Habits, however, are not fixed and static, they are mutable, they are altered in action.

A second feature common to the traditional theories must be rejected. The traditional ethical theories agree that their "business is to discover some final end or good or some ultimate and supreme law." Kantianism and utilitarianism begin with a conception of the ultimate moral good, what philosophers call the '*summum bonum*', the "highest good." According to Kant, this good is the will that is obedient to Reason; on Mill's view, it is the satisfaction of desire. For both, the *summum bonum* is fixed and final. Dewey asks:

> Is not the belief in the single, final and ultimate. . . an intellectual product of that feudal organization which is disappearing historically and of that belief in a bounded, ordered cosmos, wherein rest is higher than motion, which has disappeared from natural science? (*RP*, MW12:172-173)

The idea of a *summum bonum* is another example of philosophy's search for an immutable, an attempt to protect tradition from science.

Dewey insists that ethics cannot begin with some theoretical conception of a fixed and final *summum bonum*; rather it must start with the actual experience of the live creature. From this perspective,

> . . . we advance to a belief in a plurality of changing, moving, individualized goods and ends, and to a belief that principles, criteria, laws are intellectual instruments for analyzing individual and unique situations . . . . (*RP*, MW12:173)

A moral theory that begins with experience, with the interaction of the organism and its dynamic surroundings, abandons the project of establishing a *summum bonum*, a final moral end or aim, and takes as its objective the examination of the ways in which the live creature, through its interactions with its surroundings, realizes—that is, "constructs"[7] — goods out of existing conditions. Put most simply, a reconstructed ethics must become *experimental*, it must bring the methods employed in science to bear upon problems of human value.

An Experimental Moral Theory

The suggestion that we must adopt the methods of science in moral philosophy will appear to some as terribly crass; "the idea of actively adopting experimental method in social affairs. . . strikes most persons as a surrender of all standards and regulative authority" (*QC*, LW4:218). This reaction is evidence that "beliefs about values are pretty much in the position in which beliefs about nature were before the scientific revolution" (*QC*, LW4:204). The argument that moral philosophy cannot be based upon science fails once it is recognized that experimental method is a regulative process. Experimentalism "does not signify random and aimless action; it implies direction by ideas and knowledge"(*QC*, LW4:218).

As with his epistemology, the concept of a problematic situation forms the basis of Dewey's moral theory; an experimental theory recognizes that moral thinking arises within *situations* that are *morally* problematic. As was discussed in the preceding chapter, the term 'situation' denotes the physical *and* social context within which the human creature lives (*LI*, LW12:48). We live not only in a world of physical objects and mechanical forces; social factors—values, customs, habits—operate in the world as well. Accordingly, just as a situation can be physically disturbed and indeterminate, there can also be situations in which the *moral* factors, the values, are disordered.

In such situations, "judgment and choice are required antecedently to overt action" because "there are conflicting desires and alternative apparent goods." The situation features conflicting *values* which are not mutually satisfiable. We feel the pull of the competing values and are perplexed, "the practical meaning of the situation . . . is not self-evident." Something must be done, but any course of action will realize some particular good and suppress others; "what is needed is to find the right course of action, the right good" (*RP*, MW12:173).

Like physically problematic situations, morally problematic situations call for *inquiry*. Although the material of moral inquiry is distinct, all inquiry exhibits a basic pattern. Dewey characterizes the phases of moral inquiry thus:

> . . . observation of the detailed makeup of the situation; analysis into its diverse factors; clarification of what is obscure; discounting of the more insistent and vivid traits; tracing the consequences of the various modes of action that suggest themselves; regarding the decision reached as hypothetical and tentative until the anticipated or supposed consequences which led to its adoption have been squared with actual consequences. (*RP*, MW12:173)

Moral inquiry is the process of *resolving* conflicts within morally problematic situations. Just as each physically problematic situation is unique, every morally problematic situation is unique; every moral situation has "its own irreplaceable good." Consequently, "Morals is not a catalogue of acts nor a set of rules to be applied like drugstore prescriptions or cook-book recipes" (*RP*, MW12:177); "morality is a continuing process, not a fixed achievement" (*HC*, MW14:194). The outcome of successful moral inquiry is not a fixed moral law, but a hypothesis, a tool which one is warranted in using in future inquiry.

There might appear to be a breakdown of the analogy between scientific and moral inquiry at this point. It may be objected that whereas scientific inquiry is successful insofar as it efficiently restores order to the problematic situation, there is something beyond efficiency required for a moral inquiry to be successful. Clearly, the most expedient and efficient solution to a moral problem is not necessarily the most morally sound solution. There must be some other standard for evaluating the solution to a morally problematic situation.

Indeed there is. As in inquiry into physical matters, proposed solutions to moral situations are evaluated not only according to their ability to resolve the problem at hand, but also according to their propensity to avoid *further* difficulties. Moral inquiry fails if in addressing a current problem it subsequently generates a worse problem. Moral inquiry is successful not only in the degree to which it addresses the current problem, but also insofar as it produces conditions in which the agent is better able to act in the future. This standard is what Dewey calls "growth."

The "end" of moral inquiry is therefore not some external "good" or fixed law; "growth itself is the only moral 'end'." Growth is not an "end" in the sense of a finality, it is an "ever-enduring process of perfecting, maturing, refining" our habits (*RP*, MW12:181). Growth is thus a *progressive* concept. Morality is no longer understood in terms of obedience to a standard of value established independently of experience, nor is it a matter of conformity to traditional customs. Dewey writes:

> The bad man is the man who no matter how good he *has* been is beginning to deteriorate, to grow less good; the good man is the man who no matter how morally unworthy he *has* been is moving to become better. (*RP*, MW12: 180-181)

In this way, experimentalism makes the material of moral evaluation *prospective*.

Moral Inquiry as Social Transformation

Moral inquiry arises when the live creature is confronted with a morally problematic situation. The conflicting values which constitute the problematic aspect of the situation are socially produced; they are the habits and traditions which the agent inherits from his community. The experience of a moral problem is the experience of the breakdown of one's social inheritance. A problem arises when existing habits are not *fit* to deal with the situation; there is a conflict to which we do not know how to respond, customary modes of response will not *do*. We inquire, and thus the habits and customs generated in the past are put to the test of new experience.

An experimental ethics requires that we understand inherited customs and habits *instrumentally*—they are tentative hypotheses, tools, the products of previous inquiry. As with a scientific hypothesis, the value of a habit lies in its ability to guide future experience. Moral inquiry thus *begins* with habits and customs generated in the past; however, as inquiry is the *resolution* of a problematic situation, it *ends* with a new situation, revised habits and customs. Experimental moral inquiry thus entails the *transformation* of society. Accordingly, moral inquiry can be practiced, and growth can occur, only within a certain kind of society. In order for moral inquiry to commence, a society cannot be tenaciously committed to its own traditions, it cannot cling dogmatically to its present values as fixed and final commandments to be obeyed. Rather, it must itself be progressive, transforming, growing, reconstructing. In Dewey's terms, moral inquiry and growth can be achieved only in a society that is democratic.

Democracy as a Way of Life

> The idea of democracy is a wider and fuller idea than can be exemplified in the state even at its best. To be realized it must affect all modes of human association, the family, the school, industry, religion. (*PP*, LW2:325)

We often think of democracy as a certain form of *government* in which the general populace elects its governors. This form of government in turn implies a series of procedures and institutions: regular popular elections, universal suffrage, a free press, political parties, etc. Democracy is thus often identified with its procedural apparatus; we think of democracy simply as a "political idea," a kind of *state* (*PP*, LW2:325). Dewey believes that if we think of democracy in this way, we miss its essential meaning. Dewey promotes a "wider and fuller" conception of democracy according to which the state and its corresponding apparatus is "not the whole of democracy" (*PP*, LW2:327). On Dewey's view, democratic political institutions are "not a final end and a final value," they rather are *means* for achieving "a truly human way of living" (LW11:218).[8] That is, democracy is essentially a "social idea" (*PP*, LW2:325), a "mode of associated living" (*DE*, MW9:93). In short, democracy is a certain *kind* of community, a certain way of life.

What kind of community is a democracy? A community is not simply a group of persons "living in physical proximity"; rather, in a community, people *share* "aims, beliefs, aspirations, knowledge" (*DE*, MW9:7), they cooperatively *participate* in the common life of the group, they consciously "share experience." In this sense, democracy is the "idea of community life itself"; the "clear consciousness of a communal life, in all its implications, constitutes the idea of democracy" (*PP*, LW2:328). Hence we derive "the nature of the democratic idea in its generic social sense":

> From the standpoint of the individual, it consists in having a responsible share according to capacity in forming and directing the activities of the groups to which one belongs and in participating according to need in the values which the groups sustain. From the standpoint of the groups, it demands liberation of the potentialities of members of a group in harmony with the interests and goods which are common. (*PP*. LW2:327-328)

The essence of a democratic community, then, is individual participation in directing and forming its activities and values. In such a community, the past *as past* and tradition *as tradition* have no final authority, a democratic community is one which is continually and cooperatively *refining* its values and *redirecting* its customs to expand the degree of growth. Thus a democratic community is necessarily a *progressive* community. Through individual participation, both the individual and the community grow. That is, more interests come to be shared, there is a "widening of the area of shared concerns, and the liberation of personal capacities" (*DE*, MW9:93).

Democracy exists primarily at the most local levels of human association. Democracy does not begin with the state; rather, "Democracy must begin at home, and its home is the neighborly community" (*PP*, LW2:368). As Dewey states in his 1939 essay on "Creative Democracy—The Task Before Us" (LW14), democracy exists not in external procedures, but "in the attitudes which human beings display to one another in all the incidents and relations of daily life" (LW14:226). Dewey continues:

> . . . the heart and final guarantee of democracy is in free gatherings of neighbors on the street corner to discuss back and forth what is read in uncensored news of the day, and in gatherings of friends in the living rooms of houses and apartments to converse freely with one another. (LW14:227)

Democracy is a mode of human association, a way of life—it involves the active participation of individuals in discussion, debate, and deliberation about political affairs; it is "essentially a cooperative undertaking, one which rests upon persuasion, upon an ability to convince and be convinced by reason" (MW10:404).

Democracy requires that we collectively *inquire* into matters of shared concern and continually engage in cooperative discourse and reasoned debate. Given its demands, the "democratic road is the hard one to take" because it "places the greatest burden of responsibility upon the greatest number of human beings" (*FC*, LW13:154). More than this, democracy requires that we practice a certain *kind* of discourse and engage in a certain *kind* of deliberation. In democratic discourse, ideas are advanced and examined according solely to the evidence that can be marshaled in their support; conclusions and decisions are taken to be tentative hypotheses, proposals for action, subject to the test of future experience and hence to revision; social status and privilege are as irrelevant as is rhetorical skill.[9] In other words, "The future of democracy is allied with the spread of the scientific attitude" (*FC*, LW13:168). The democratic way of life requires that we model our public discourse upon the experimental method of science. Particularly, we must adopt the "attitude" and "morale" of scientific inquiry, which Dewey characterizes thus:

> Some of its obvious elements are willingness to hold belief in suspense, ability to doubt until evidence is obtained; willingness to go where the evidence points instead of putting first a personally preferred conclusion; ability to hold ideas in solution and use them as hypotheses to be tested instead of as dogmas to be asserted; and . . . enjoyment of new fields for inquiry and of new problems. (*FC*, LW13:166)

Democracy requires "the improvement of the methods and conditions of debate, discussion and persuasion" (*PP*, LW2:365). In his day, Dewey was concerned about the increasing power of media to "undermine democracy from within" through propaganda, the creation of "pseudo-public opinion" (*FC*, LW13:168).[10] Today, it is difficult not to be more pessimistic than Dewey with regard to the prospects of public deliberation.[11] Yet Dewey insists that democracy as a way of life also entails a "faith in the capacities of human nature; faith in human intelligence, and in the power of pooled, cooperative experience" (LW11:219). To accept this is to realize that the barriers to realizing the democratic way of life exist "*within* our own institutions and attitudes." "The struggle for democracy," Dewey writes,

> . . . can be won only by extending the application of democratic methods, methods of consultation, persuasion, negotiation, communication, cooperative intelligence, in the task of making our own politics, industry, education, our culture generally, a servant and an evolving manifestation of democratic ideas. (*FC*, LW13:187)

According to Dewey, the democratic way of life can be realized only through the adoption and expansion of the democratic attitude and experimental method in all of our social institutions and associations. Currently, our workplaces, our schools, and our public spaces are dominated by dogmatism and authoritarianism; our political ideas and social ideals come pre-packaged in marketing images and infectious slogans and sound-bites. Within this scene, the critical inquiry and deliberative discussion necessary to democratic growth are discouraged—we are told to "just do it" (what?) or to pledge obedience to some other external power.

To further the democratic project, we must reconstruct and rehabilitate existing social conditions. Our schools must cease being centers for job training where individuals go to acquire mechanical skills; they must become centers of cooperative *inquiry* in the fullest sense of the term. Similarly, our workplaces must be transformed from hierarchical power structures organized according to profit-minded management theory to scenes of cooperative endeavor and shared effort. Our families and households, too, must exhibit the qualities of democratic community. Lastly, each of us must attempt to bring the method of experimental inquiry to bear upon our own lives, commitments, beliefs, and values; moreover, the spirit of cooperative discourse must animate our relations with others.

Summary

Modern Moral philosophy features a dualism between "inner" motives and "outer" actions. From the standpoint of the live creature, such a dualism is untenable. Dewey proposes an experimental ethics which emphasizes the process of moral *inquiry*. The creature engages in moral inquiry when confronted with a situation which features conflicting values, and the process of resolving moral problems follows the general pattern of inquiry discussed in Chapter Five.

On Dewey's theory, morality has to do with refining, revising, and correcting habitual patterns of behavior inherited from society. The agent is said to have "grown" in the degree to which present inquiry has helped solidify and enable habits that contribute positively to future behavior. Moral inquiry thus involves the gradual reconstruction of social practices and customs. Such inquiry can be practiced only within a community that is itself committed to growth as a progressive ideal. Democracy is the idea of such a community.

The term 'democracy' does not denote simply a series of familiar political procedures; democracy is rather a way of life. The democratic way of life is that of applying the methods of experimental inquiry, and cooperative, critical discourse to every form of human association. Democracy as a way of life is therefore a continuing project of promoting the growth of each individual through the democratic reconstruction of all social institutions.

Endnotes

[1] Citations to Kant will be drawn from *Foundations of the Metaphysics of Morals* (New York: Macmillan Publishing, 1985).
[2] More correctly, they are transcendental or "noumenal."
[3] Kant is not disturbed by this implication: "Our concern is with actions of which perhaps the world has never had an example..." (24).
[4] For this criticism, see Hegel's *Phenomenology of Spirit* (Oxford: Oxford University Press, 1977), 365ff.
[5] Citations to Mill are drawn from *Utilitarianism* (Indianapolis: Hackett, 1979).
[6] Hence Mill: ". . . the sole evidence it is possible to produce that anything is desirable is the people do actually desire it" (34). Compare Dewey, "the fact that something is desired only raises the *question* of its desirability; it does not settle it" (*QC*, LW4:208).
[7] One of Dewey's most important statements of his moral philosophy is the tenth chapter of *The Quest for Certainty* (LW4), which is aptly entitled "The Construction of Good" (*QC*, LW4:203-228).
[8] The quotes are drawn from Dewey's 1937 address, "Democracy and Educational Administration" (LW11:217-225).
[9] See Sidney Hook's essays, "The Democratic Way of Life," in his *Reason, Social Myths, and Democracy* (New York: Prometheus Books, 1991), and his "The Ethics of Controversy," in his *Philosophy and Public Policy* (Carbondale: Southern Illinois University Press, 1980) for characteristically elegant expressions of the Deweyan view.
[10] See also *FC*, LW13:156 and *PP*, LW2:348-349.
[11] See, for example, Edward Herman and Noam Chomsky's *Manufacturing Consent* (New York: Pantheon Books, 1988), Douglas Kellner's *Television and the Crisis of Democracy* (Colorado: Westview Press, 1990), and Benjamin Page's *Who Deliberates?* (Illinois: University of Chicago Press, 1998) for contemporary analyses of media and propaganda.

6
A Prospective Conclusion

The very notion of a conclusion that is *prospective*, forward looking, may seem paradoxical. The conclusion of a book typically consists in a grand summing-up of the ground that has been covered in the preceding pages. No study of Dewey's thought can have a conclusion in this ordinary sense. Not unlike democracy itself, Dewey's philosophy is a continuing project, a process of growth, a vision of what we can become.

Therefore, Dewey's achievement lies not in his scholarly *corpus*, but in the power of his example. Living by Dewey's example consists not simply in studying his works and composing academic articles and books (like this one) about his ideas. Such activities can at the very best serve an intermediary function of calling others to the challenge of realizing Dewey's vision; at worst (and most often), they become a comfortable, safe substitute for that project.

Dewey's example requires nothing short of dedicating one's life to the extension of the application of democratic intelligence to every aspect of human association. As the social institutions that currently dominate our lives—our schools, our workplaces, our households—are most often decidedly anti-democratic, our mission is not easily met. The task before us requires a myriad of virtues: courage, integrity, honesty, and dedication. Perhaps the most difficult requirements are those of the willingness to cooperate with others in the face of difference and opposition, the strength to persist in pursuit of envisioned ideal, and the drive to realize a shared future out of a fragmented present. Of course, inspiration is also necessary to the project, and maybe even a certain faith in the possibility of its success.

You may in the future find yourself in Burlington, Vermont. If so, make your way to Ira Allen Chapel on University Place. Although originally used for religious services, the Chapel now serves as a center for public lectures, concerts, and other community activities. It is in many ways a fitting place for a memorial to John Dewey. The modest stone marking the resting place of the ashes of John Dewey bears an inscription from his 1934 book, *A Common Faith.* The full quotation cannot be bettered as a statement of Dewey's faith in the human community, in us.

> We who now live are parts of a humanity that has interacted with nature. The things in civilization we most prize are not of ourselves. They exist by grace of the doings and sufferings of the continuous human community in which we are a link. Ours is the responsibility of conserving, transmitting, rectifying, and expanding the heritage of values we have received that those who come after us may receive it more solid and secure, more widely accessible and more generously shared than we have received it. Here are all the elements for a religious faith that shall not be confined to sect, class, or race. Such a faith has always been implicitly the common faith of mankind. It remains to make it explicit and militant. (*CF*, LW9: 57-58)

Suggestions for Further Reading

Complete bibliographical information for Dewey's *Works* is given below (section A). I also have included information about the standard anthologies of Dewey's writings (section B). The mountain of literature on John Dewey continues to enlarge at an amazing rate; in section C, I have suggested some of the more accessible secondary works. The list is not intended to be a comprehensive bibliography of the recent literature, and, with one exception, I have limited the suggestions to only those books that are still in print. Suggestions regarding more advanced studies of Dewey's thought and relevant literature concerning other philosophers have been mentioned in the endnotes and are therefore not included here.

A. Critical Editions of Dewey's Writings

Dewey, John. *The Early Works of John Dewey, 1882-1898.* Edited by Jo Ann Boydston. 5 vols. Carbondale: Southern Illinois University Press, 1969-1972.

________. *The Middle Works of John Dewey, 1899-1924.* Edited by Jo Ann Boydston. 15 vols. Carbondale: Southern Illinois University Press, 1976-1983.

________. *The Later Works of John Dewey, 1925-1953.* Edited by Jo Ann Boydston. 17 vols. Carbondale: Southern Illinois University Press, 1981-1990.

B. Edited Collections of Dewey's Writings

Hickman, Larry and Alexander, Thomas, eds. *The Essential Dewey.* 2 vols. Indiana: Indiana University Press, 1998.

McDermott, John, ed. *The Philosophy of John Dewey.* Illinois: University of Chicago Press, 1973.

C. Recommended Secondary Works on Dewey

Biographical

Dykhuizen, George. *The Life and Mind of John Dewey.* Illinois: Southern Illinois University Press, 1973.

Rockefeller, Stephen. *John Dewey: Religious Faith and Democratic Humanism.* New York: Columbia University Press, 1991.

Ryan, Alan. *John Dewey and the High Tide of American Liberalism.* New York: W. W. Norton, 1995.

Westbrook, Robert. *John Dewey and American Democracy.* Ithaca, New York: Cornell University Press, 1991.

Philosophical

Bernstein, Richard. *John Dewey.* California: Ridgeview Publishing Company, 1966.

Campbell, James. *Understanding John Dewey.* Illinois: Open Court, 1995.

Eldridge, Michael. *Transforming Experience: John Dewey's Cultural Instrumentalism.* Nashville: Vanderbilt University Press, 1998.

Hickman, Larry, ed. *Reading Dewey: Interpretations for a Postmodern Generation.* Indiana: Indiana University Press, 1998.

Hook, Sidney. *John Dewey: An Intellectual Portrait.* New York: John Day Co, 1939. Reprinted with a new introduction by Richard Rorty by Prometheus Books (New York: Prometheus Books, 1995).

Schilpp Paul A. and Hahn, Lewis, eds. *The Philosophy of John Dewey.* Volume 1 of the *Library of Living Philosophers.* Illinois: Open Court, 1989.